play like
John Mayer

Audio
PLAYBACK
Speed · Pitch · Balance · Loop

MW00579857

The Ultimate Guitar Lesson

by Jeff Adams

To access audio visit:
www.halleonard.com/mylibrary

Enter Code
8512-6315-6921-1935

Cover photo: © JeromeBrunet.com

ISBN 978-1-4950-1697-4

EXCLUSIVELY DISTRIBUTED BY

7777 W. BLUEMOUND RD. P.O. BOX 13819 MILWAUKEE, WI 53213

In Australia Contact:
Hal Leonard Australia Pty. Ltd.
4 Lentara Court
Cheltenham, Victoria, 3192 Australia
Email: ausadmin@halleonard.com.au

Visit Hal Leonard Online at
www.halleonard.com

CONTENTS

INTRODUCTION

John Mayer's boyish heartthrob looks, expressive vocals, and thoughtful songwriting made him a household name in the pop world of the early 2000s, but his incredible guitar playing has since certified him as an authentic master of the instrument. His ability to expound on the licks of his guitar heroes—including B.B. King, Buddy Guy, Eric Clapton, Jimi Hendrix, and Stevie Ray Vaughan, to name a few—and deftly apply them to pop structures has garnered him both public and critical acclaim.

Much like SRV amidst the then-popular music backdrop of '80s metal, Mayer allows his blues roots to inform the R&B/funk influences of his commercial hits. Even though he's not writing a straight-ahead, 12-bar blues that becomes a chart-topping success, he brings the guitar to the forefront of popular music with blues phrasing, melodic soloing, and technical intrigue.

A rare breed of accomplished guitar player that considers himself a songwriter above all else, John's pragmatic approach to his career has led him to corral his writing, musicianship, and arranging skills to be perpetually listenable. As a result, his studio albums perfectly balance art and commerce, while his live albums show off his arranging creativity. However, the through line of all this musical output is his incendiary guitar playing, which pays homage to his influences and is purified by his signature melodic sense.

This installment of Hal Leonard's *Play Like* series endeavors to show how John Mayer's eclectic guitar style and informed songwriting reinvigorated popular music of the 2000s with elements of '70s funk, '80s blues, and '90s R&B. The songs, licks, and lessons in this extensive volume are particularly focused on his blues-based, melodic guitar playing and in-depth songwriting process, so welcome to this exhaustive look into John Mayer's multifaceted artistry.

ABOUT THE AUDIO

To hear the audio examples that accompany this book, simply go to **www.halleonard.com/mylibrary** and enter the code found on page 1. This will grant you instant access to every audio track, for download or streaming. The examples that include audio are marked with an audio icon throughout the book.

NOTABLE EQUIPMENT

The connection between player and instrument becomes one of the most powerful relationships in the world of music. How hard your fingers fret the strings, how your strumming variations create vibrations through the strings to the body of the guitar, and how that resonance yields a particular tone is a truly personal affair that can inspire creativity in the most unexpected of ways. Mayer experiences this on a daily basis where his guitars, amps, and even pedals have unleashed his creative energy. Check out the footnotes for each piece of gear as they detail the role it had to play.

With a massive collection of over 200 guitars, John brings 40 of them on the road. He plays 10 to 15 songs a night, so his love affair with the instrument is well-nurtured. He's stated that he plays the same instrument he used on the album in his live shows, so his concerts are a good barometer for what instrument he used on the record.

His guitar technician is Rene Martinez, the esteemed luthier and amp guru whom maintained the legendary axes and amps of the explosive bluesman Stevie Ray Vaughan. He's been quoted as saying, "he's [John] the only guy who can make it sound worth [anything]," as he's setting up SRV's "Lenny" reproduction model, Custom Shop guitar. This seal of approval from SRV's former tech is a testament to John's skill as a guitarist and authenticity as a bluesman.

To help us save trees, as well as your precious learning time, we'll restrict our examination to the pieces relevant to the songs within this collection. I'll only spark your gear-lust with this chapter, so for those of you wanting to venture down the rabbit hole of John's enviable collection, the internet awaits your curiosity.

Guitars

With Stevie Ray Vaughan, Jimi Hendrix, Eric Clapton, and Buddy Guy as primary influences, John Mayer's guitar of choice has gravitated towards the Fender Stratocaster. His large hands and powerful attack has him rely on large frets, a wide neck, thick strings, and a sanded down finish. Removing the lacquer not only helps with the speed of the neck in humid climates, but it allows the wood of the body to resonate with great results. All these elements add up to a huge *acoustic* tone from the instrument, and the electronics that follow only attempt to faithfully represent it.

- **Fender Artist Series Stevie Ray Vaughan Signature Stratocaster (cherry sunburst, 1996—SN6940522)**: In 1996, John traded a Takamine 12-string and a Mesa Boogie distortion pedal with $900 cash to acquire this guitar. Now road-worn and his most prized instrument, John's alterations include a red tortoise shell pickguard, the left-handed whammy bar, and a custom engraved neck plate.
  Songs: "Slow Dancing In a Burning Room"

- **Fender Custom Shop Stratocaster—"Black1" (black, 2004)**: In October 2004, he visited Fender's Custom Shop and personally used their machinery to shape and sand the wood of the neck and body, putting on all the finishing touches of the instrument to fulfill his grade-school dream of building his own guitar. Due to the wood's curing process at the Fender factory, the days he spent at the Corona, CA facility were followed by a month-long wait for the instrument to arrive at his apartment in late November. The anticipation was met with dismay when he first plugged it in. After he fixed a grounding weld that wasn't sealed properly, however, the guitar came alive with a dramatically resonant tone. The guitar, with its fourth-position pickup "from heaven," went on to inspire monumental titles from *Continuum*, such as "I Don't Trust Myself (With Loving You)" and "Gravity."

- **Fender Artist Series John Mayer Signature Stratocaster**: Inspired by his modified SRV Stratocaster, John Mayer collaborated with Fender to create this signature guitar. With similar dimensions and wood choices as the SRV model, the John Mayer Signature Strat uniquely features Big Dipper pickups, tonally modified with a special mid-range scoop. As of his 2014 split with Fender, these Strats are becoming a rare find.

- **Martin OMJM John Mayer Special Edition Signature Acoustic**: After John's single, "No Such Thing," became a bona fide hit, Martin approached him to create a limited run of high-end signature acoustic guitars in 2003. The resulting OM-28JM model quickly sold out of the 404 instruments, which clearly established high demand for the artist's namesake guitar. So in 2005, a full-on production run of his signature OMJM guitar became available, featuring less ornate inlays to create a beautifully affordable instrument.

- **Fender Custom Shop Jimi Hendrix Monterey Pop Stratocaster**
  Songs: "Waiting on the World to Change" and "Bold as Love"

- **Fender Custom Shop La Cabronita Especial Telecaster**
  Songs: "Perfectly Lonely"

- **Gibson Custom ES-335 1959 Neck VOS Electric Guitar**: Possibly a Clapton-inspired purchase, the guitar is quite similar to the one he used from his days with Cream.
  Songs: "Try"

- **Martin DM3MD Dave Matthews Signature Acoustic**: This guitar was used in the promotional tour for the album *Room for Squares*, so it's plausible this is what he played on that album.

- **Strings**: A D'Addario endorsee, John relies on their durability and consistency for all his workhorse guitars. His heavier gauge electric guitar strings (EXL115: 0.011s) withstand his aggressive right-hand techniques, and his medium acoustic strings (EXP16: 0.012s) pair beautifully with his smaller body, orchestra model guitars.

- **Picks**: Dunlop Tortex, Pitch Black (0.60mm).

Amps

No slouch in the amp collector's department, Mayer's high-end boutique tube amps are pushed to their limit for warm sustain and dynamic attack for an inspired blues tone.

- **Two-Rock John Mayer Signature Head (100 Watts)**: Set to John's specifications, this limited run of only 25 amps is based on the company's still-available Custom Reverb Amp, so the tone isn't quite out of reach.

- **Dumble "Steel-String Singer" Amp Head (150 Watts)**: The reclusive electronics guru, Alexander "Howard" Dumble, became notorious in the '80s for the secretive distortion circuits in his coveted boutique amplifiers—he even covers the electronics in epoxy, so the circuit boards would be destroyed if ever removed. The word-of-mouth that spread for their amazing tone inspired artists like Santana, Robben Ford, Eric Johnson, Stevie Ray Vaughan, and more to fanatically add the amps to their backlines. Fewer than 300 of these legendary amps actually exist, and they're outrageously expensive because of that fact. Fortunately, John was able to acquire this Steel-String Singer from Jackson Browne.

- **Fender Bandmaster Head**

- **Alessandro Speaker Cabinets**: John plugs the three aforementioned amp heads into four of these speaker cabinets for their "blues" tone.

- **Hammond Leslie Rotary Speaker**: This classic amp effect features a rotating speaker, creating a rapid fluctuation in pitch. This swirling sound can be heard in the tone of Mayer's solo from "Perfectly Lonely."

- **Mesa Boogie Cabinet**

Effects

With the amps providing the majority of his tone, the effects John uses are more of an icing on his sonic cake. He uses overdrives as a boost for his solo tone, the modulation pedals are characteristic of some of his signature licks, and delays provide an ever-present feeling of ambient depth.

- **AdrenaLinn I, II, and III**: This multi-effects looper pedal allows you to input licks and sync them to the unit's internal drum machine. The sound of the programmed, single-note lines is its legacy, and Mayer's use immortalized it in songs like "Bigger Than My Body," "I Don't Trust Myself (With Loving You)," and "Heartbreak Warfare." The settings John specifically used on each of these songs can be found in each of the pedals' FAQ sections at *www.rogerlinndesign.com*.

- **Ibanez TS808 Tube Screamer**: His main overdrive pedal, John sets the drive to around 11 o'clock with the volume to the desired level. Because his amps are already quite loud, the TS808 functions as a sustain pedal more than anything else.

- **Pete Cornish NG-2**: The bizarre filtering of this distortion pedal inspired the feel of John's "Crossroads" cover from *Battle Studies*.

- **Keeley Katana Boosts**: He's been seen kicking this on for an extra solo boost.

- **Klon Centaur**

- **Way Huge "Aqua Puss" Delay**

- **Marshall Bluesbreaker MK1**

- **RMC8-Guitar Eqwahlyzer**: This versatile wah-wah pedal features a five-band EQ for controlling the tone of the sweep.

- **Custom Audio Electronics Switching System**: Designed by Bob Bradshaw to seamlessly interface with all of Mayer's amps and effects, this system consists of a MIDI controller and various bypass components that allow John to switch preset combinations of his analog effects with the push of one button. While it's not a must-have for the home player, it's invaluable in enabling John to recreate his studio sound in a live setting.

SONGS

In this chapter, we're going to look at five songs that collectively chronicle John Mayer's growth as an artist. Throughout his career, he's covered a vast amount of musical ground, including acoustic-heavy songcraft, melodic blues, and faithful emulations of his influences. This section puts all those styles on display.

Each song features an accompanying lesson that explains the techniques he uses to play the song and the songwriting concepts that bring it to life. While photos and tab examples sufficiently explain the physical techniques, some of the songwriting concepts are abstract and theory-heavy. It would be a disservice to John's artistry to exclude these concepts, so the headier of these ideas are enclosed in gray boxes throughout.

No Such Thing
From *Room for Squares*, 2001

John Mayer's debut album was an unexpected, instant success for the 25-year-old. Recorded over the course of two months in New York and Maryland (commencing a mere two days after he signed the record contract), *Room for Squares* went on to sell three million copies with easy-listening, acoustic-driven songs like the Grammy Award-winning "Your Body Is a Wonderland" and the introspective "Why Georgia."

"No Such Thing" was the first single off the record and placed on display his penchant for lyrically finding the slice of life we've all experienced but can't explain. Framed by a retrospective look at his high school experiences in Fairfield, CT, the lyrics bring to light the fallibility of following the status quo versus following your passions. Passed over by many as a generic pop song, the brilliant concepts contained within show off John's often-unsung songwriting chops. Of course, we'll give him his due credit here. For reference, the song transcription begins on page 12.

Intro

The intro is essentially an eight-measure, I chord vamp, in which Mayer uses interesting thematic approaches to build into the main groove. Starting out on acoustic (Gtr. 1), his chord choices are unconventional to the average rhythm player. Where most would opt for the vanilla, open-E chord, Mayer chooses Emaj9 and Eadd9 voicings at the 11th position. Although the chord names sound complicated, they're quite simple to grab and sound great in this context.

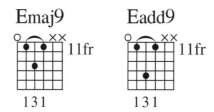

While Mayer plays these chords with his index and ring fingers, economy of motion suggests that you use your pinky finger at the 14th fret for the Eadd9 chord.

True to his rhythm playing form, Mayer's right hand alternates between single-string palm muting and chord stabs on beat 2 and the "and" of beats 3 and 4. This, coupled with the chord changes every two measures, rounds out the hypnotic groove and creates a solid foundation for the song.

At measure 4, a clean tone electric (Gtr. 2) enters with an E octave-shape texture. Although convention dictates to mute the in-between string for unruly notes, this carefully selected open string is B, the 5th of the underlying E harmony, so its ringing character is a welcome addition to the harmony. This juxtaposition of fretted notes and open strings allows for a mixture of pleasingly round, yet bright sounds. Atop this sonic intrigue, he plays an E–D♯–E–B line derived from the Emaj9 harmony to close out the intro.

Verse

Here the bass and drums enter (with the drums entering a measure later than the bass in an interesting production choice), and Gtr. 1 continues on with its rhythmic MO, applying other extended chord shapes to the I–IV–vi–i progression of measures 9–16.

The Emaj9 (Imaj9) and Amaj9 (IVmaj9) chords are quite similar shapes, but the Amaj9 is moved up a string set and takes advantage of the open B and E strings for that 9th sound.

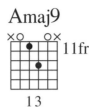

The C♯m11 (vi) throws in our first technical hairball: *thumb fretting.* John Mayer, like his influences, Stevie Ray Vaughan and Jimi Hendrix, has huge hands, so he simply curls his thumb over the back of the neck and grabs the ninth fret of the E string (C♯) as his remaining fingers do the rest.

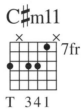

Slowly switching between the Amaj9 and C♯m11 chords, with no rhythm, is a great way to get your thumb in gear. Take note of how your hand feels in the process, though, as the last thing you want is a nasty case of tendonitis. (For more info on safe practice, check out the Thumb Fretting section on page 106.) Another way to fret this chord is to replace your thumb with your middle finger, so there are options beyond the pain.

The Em11–Em7–Em9 sequence in measures 15 and 16 (collectively serving as the i chord) has three interesting musical concepts at work: *voice leading, parallel harmony,* and *word painting.* These concepts get sequentially more abstract and build on each other, so let's get the physical barriers of playing the chords out of the way first.

They start out as 10th-position, G5/E chords with the low-E string serving as the root.

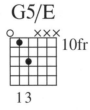

By simply adding your pinky to the G string for the 14th and 12th frets and then utilizing your middle finger for the 11th fret, you get an economic chord sequence featuring harmonic movement.

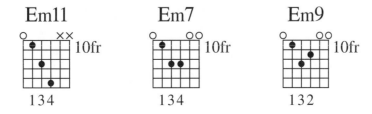

How these chords get their names is through the *voice leading* that happens to match his descending vocal line. As he's singing A–G–F♯ for the lyrics, "*Plot* it *out* in *black* and white" (italics denote changes in pitch), the Em11 chord he plays on beats 1 and 2 has an *A* note on top (11th), Em7 on the "and" of beat 3 has a *G* on top (♭3rd), and the Em9 on the "and" of beat 4 has an *F♯* on top (9th).

While the first three chords (I–IV–vi) are part of the standard pop songwriting formula, the use of the i minor chord (E minor sequence in measures 15–16) is an underutilized concept of classical music known as *parallel harmony*. Simply put, if E major and E minor chords are used in the same song, they are said to have parallel harmony because they have the same root letter with different *qualities* (e.g., major and minor).

Now, the E minor sequence is specifically used for another concept called *word painting*. This refers to a songwriting approach where the intent of the lyrics is supported with the mood or flow of the music. Since minor chords have the sonic quality of a "saddening" of the mood, the lyrics must reflect that for word painting to be present.

So, what do we know about the story of the song? Well, Mayer has said that the message is to take the road less traveled, even though authority figures have said otherwise. With this in mind, let's take a look at the lyrics of the first eight measures of the verse. The lyrics start with him sitting in a female guidance counselor's office where she's encouraging him to think about his future:

"Welcome to the real world," she said to me,
Condescendingly.
"Take a seat, take your life.

And on the E minor chord sequence, she says...

Plot it out in black and white."

Here, the "saddening" of the mood is evident where she challenges him to make a choice about things of which he is uncertain. This specific chord sequence can be thought of as an "uncertainty" motif. Is that a stretch? Well, let's take a look at the 2nd verse lyrics. Here, Mayer is reflecting on the irony of how his fellow students whom followed the counselor's advice were as insecure as he is.

So the good boys and girls take the so-called right track,
Faded white hats, grabbing credits, and maybe transfers.

And on the E minor chord sequences, he opines...

They read all the books but they can't find the answers.

Again, we see the word painting concept at work—answers out of reach for the "good boys and girls" who stayed within the status quo. A melancholy statement for their unrealized dreams, supported by a *parallel minor* chord to enhance the *word painting* concept—all in a pop song! All three of these songwriting and melodic devices superbly round out the first eight measures of the verse.

While measures 17–22 maintain the I–IV–vi sequence, measures 23 and 24 introduce a deviation from the E minor sequence. Instead of a i chord, he closes the verse with an F♯7 sequence (F♯7♭5–F♯7–F♯9). Once again, these extensions are simply a voice leading device that follows the vocal line (C♮–C♯–G♯), but the grips are not as simple. They require thumb fretting and careful patience for all the notes to clearly ring. To see the voice leading at work, here's the underlying shape.

F♯7

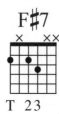

T 23

Here's how Mayer pulls them off. He adds his index finger to the B string on the first fret, shifts that finger to the second fret, and then adds his pinky to the fourth fret of the E string.

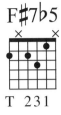

F#7♭5

T 2 3 1

F#7

T 2 3 1
T 1 3 2
T 1 2 1

F#9

T 2 3 1 4
T 1 3 2 4
T 1 2 1 4

Note that it's very difficult to grab the F#9 the way Mayer does unless you have large hands. To make the fingering a little more manageable, check out the two sets of alternate fingerings shown for the F#7 and F#9 chords. (The second set of alternate fingerings includes a partial barre with the index finger.) These allow for a little more curling motion of the wrist to let all the notes ring.

This second half of verse 2 (measures 53–60) grows in arrangement in a similar manner as the intro with the addition of Gtr. 2. Here, the E-octave motif from the intro is restated in an arpeggiated manner to match the rhythmic accents of Gtr. 1. While the E, B, and D# notes of the riff work with the Emaj9, Amaj9, and C#m11 chords, take note of how he modifies it to fit the F#7 sequence at the end of the verse by adding an A# note (3rd of F#) to the mix.

Pre-Chorus

Here, the drums move from the verse's *backbeat* groove (snare hits on 2 and 4) to adding quarter-note hi-hat hits. Mayer reacts to this by modifying his pattern from offbeat accents to a more aggressive eighth- and sixteenth-note strumming pattern for the pair of six-measure phrases of the pre-chorus.

For the confusing-looking A-chord sequence of measures 25–28 (Asus2–A6/9–Asus2–Amaj9), Mayer is cleverly reinforcing his vocal line with his guitar part. As his vocals ascend the E major pentatonic scale (E–F#–G#–B), he moves a power chord shape on strings 4 and 3—in conjunction with the surrounding open A, B, and E strings—up along with it, so that the note on string 4 largely doubles his vocal line. (The one exception is the G# note in the vocal, which is matched with an A note on string 4.) This demonstrates an effective method for creating a bit of movement during a long portion of *static harmony* (i.e., one chord).

In the following chord frames, in addition to the full chord names, each power chord shape is shown as it relates to the open A string.

(E5/A)
Asus2

1 4

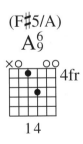

(F#5/A)
A$_9^6$
4fr

1 4

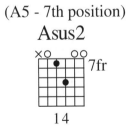

(A5 - 7th position)
Asus2
7fr

1 4

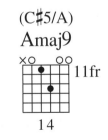

(C#5/A)
Amaj9
11fr

1 4

After reverting to the accented Emaj9 chord rhythm for measures 29 and 30, measures 31–35 move through simple chord grips with eighth-note strumming that ends on an accented "and" of beat 4 to anticipate the chorus. Here are the F#11 and E/G# shapes—the only ones we haven't encountered so far.

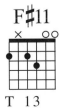

F#11

T 1 3

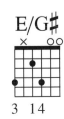

E/G#

3 1 4

Chorus

After his two-beat vocal anticipation into the chorus, Gtr. 1 enters with a two-measure Am11–D7sus4–Emaj9 chord progression that loops the entire section until he sustains the Emaj9 chord on the "and" of beat 4 in measure 43. The Am11 chord is the same shape and fingering as the C#m11 chord found in the verse, but its root is on the fifth fret, so the shape should be comfortable by now. The following D7sus4 chord is a 10th-position, Hendrix-style voicing that comfortably moves to the 11th-position Emaj9 on the "and" of beat 4.

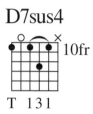

The somewhat complex-looking tablature like that seen in measures 37 and 39 is simply getting very specific with what sections of strings he's playing at any given moment. As a rhythm player, it's easier to think of the tab where you're reading the rhythms rather than the confusing inconsequential details. Therefore, the same chorus riff could be represented as follows:

No Such Thing
Example 1

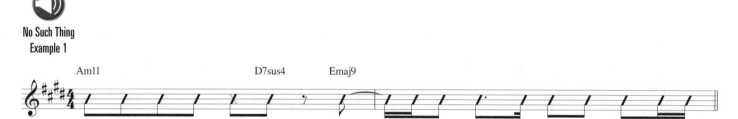

Coming along for the ride is Gtr. 2, obstinately hammering away at an E-octave shape for the entirety of the chorus as a constant pedal tone, helping to anchor the song's harmony amidst the wandering iv–♭VII7–I progression.

Bridge

After the verse and chorus are played again, we come across the bridge section. Commonly called "the middle eight," this section serves to lyrically and/or melodically expand upon the song's material and often shed new light on the chorus's lyrics. The statement of "I am invincible as long as I'm alive" is cliché enough, but the music under it is rife with musical interest.

The *half-time feel* (drums only accent beat 3 to make two measures sound like one) provides a striking contrast to the constant eighth-note pulse of the first 2-1/2 minutes. The Fmaj7#11 and Aadd9 chords are deceptively simple grips, based on the sixth-string, major barre chord shape. Once again, Mayer takes advantage of the open B and E strings to create the harmonic intrigue. The G13 chord that ends the bridge is another simple grip, but his use of the thumb on the third fret of the E string potentially complicates things for those with smaller hands. Try the alternate fingering shown if John's preferred method doesn't sit well with you.

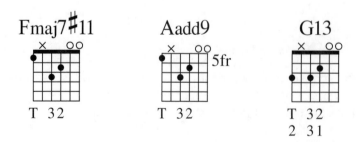

Harmonically, the G13 change helps propel us out of the bridge (with the aid of the drums) and into the interlude, ending the half-time feel.

Note: Another rabbit trail of parallel minor analysis can be applied here, but suffice it to say that the Fmaj7#11 and G9 chords are borrowed from an A minor tonality.

Outro

Gtr. 2 rejoins at the outro for an interesting arpeggio figure that moves through G♯m (a.k.a. the top triad of Emaj7), Esus4, E, and Esus2 chord shapes at the 11th position.

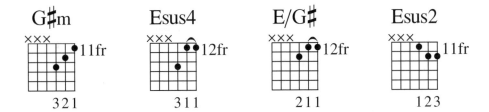

Gtr. 3 takes more of a passive role by sustaining a beautiful Emaj9 voicing. Even though he mutes the fifth-string note, here's the grip in its entirety.

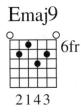

NO SUCH THING

Words and Music by John Mayer and Clay Cook

No Such Thing
Full Song

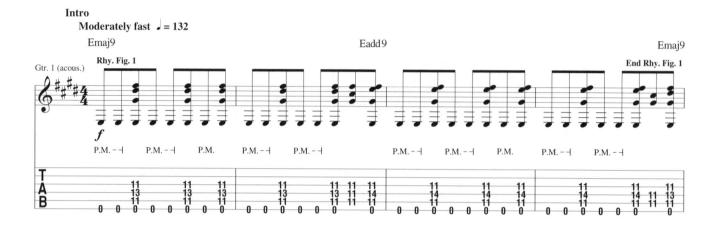

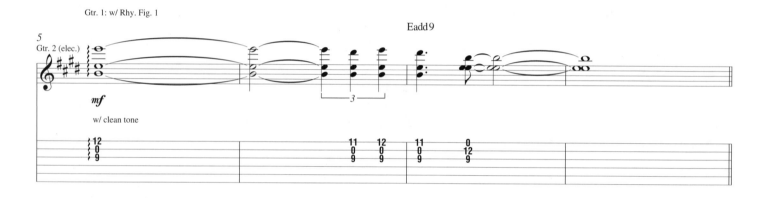

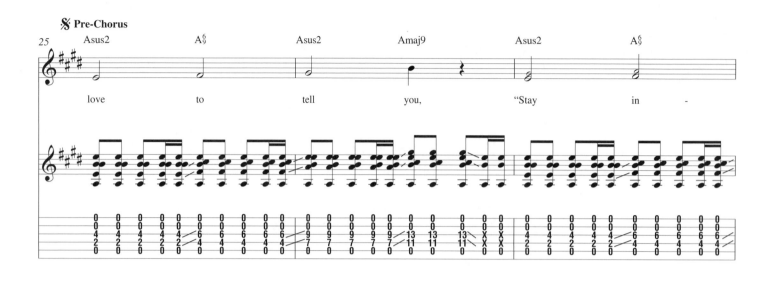

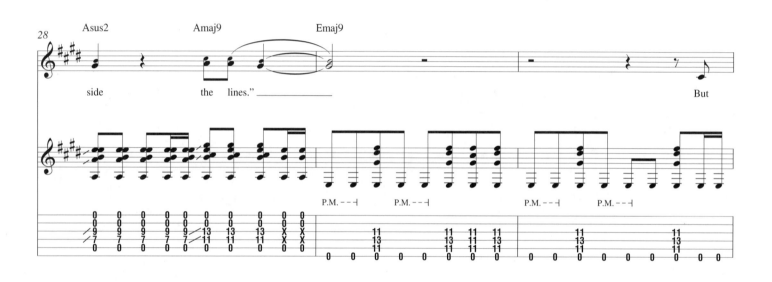

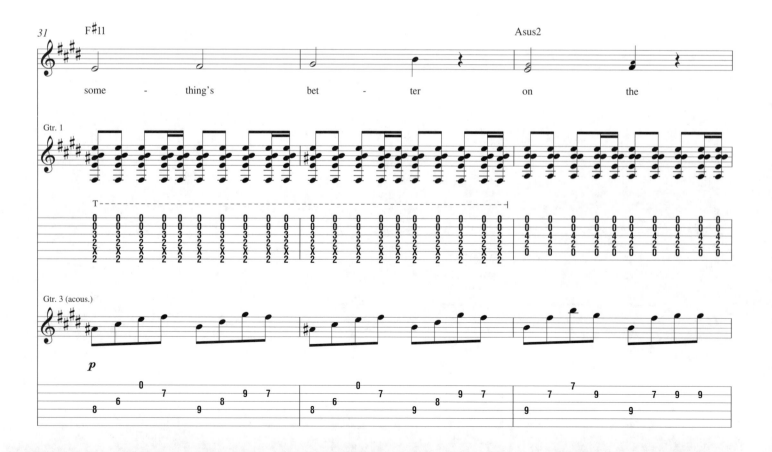

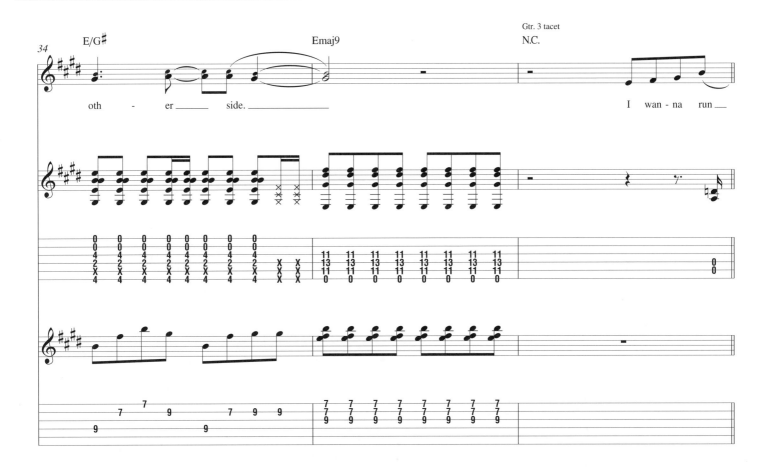

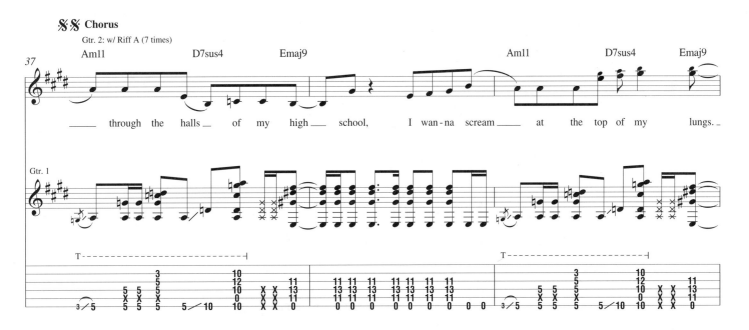

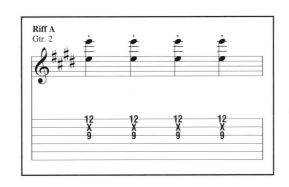

To Coda 1 ⊕
To Coda 2 ⊕

D.S. al Coda 1

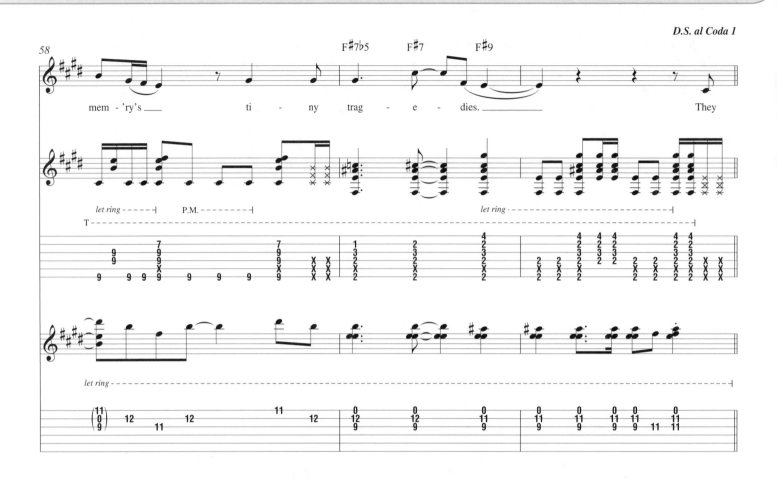

Coda 1

Bridge
Half-time feel

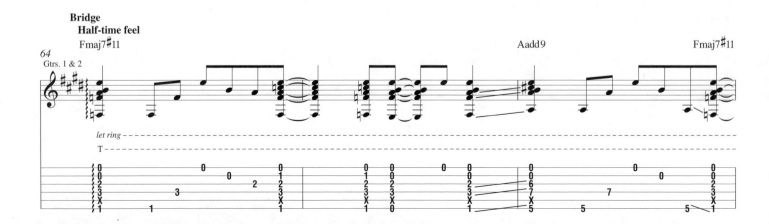

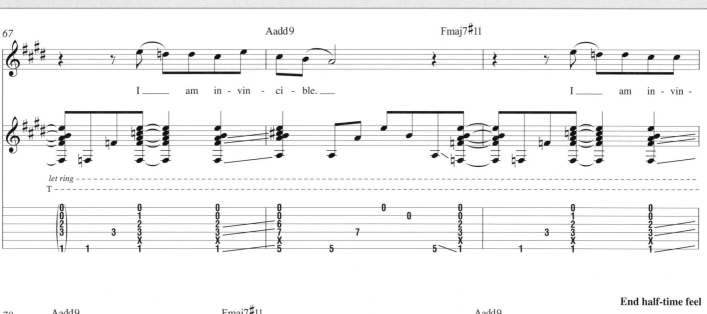

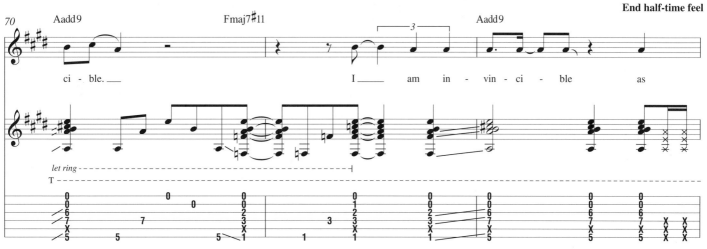

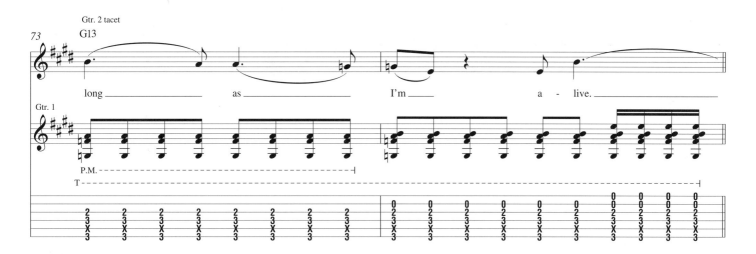

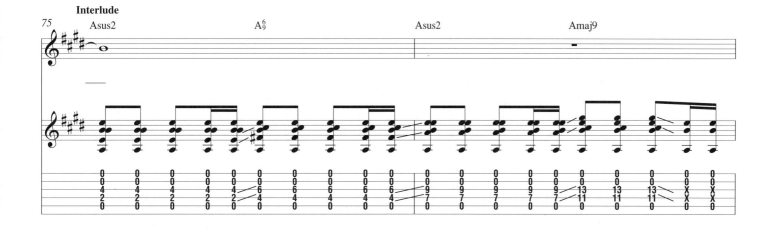

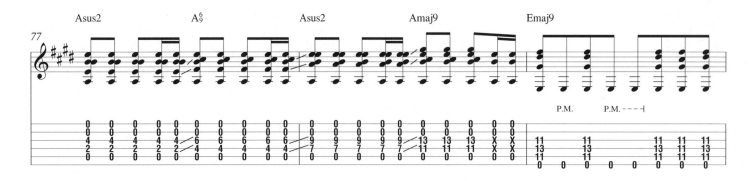

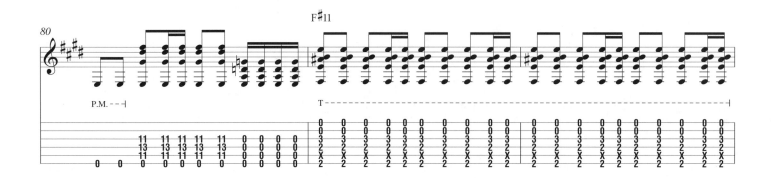

D.S.S. al Coda 2

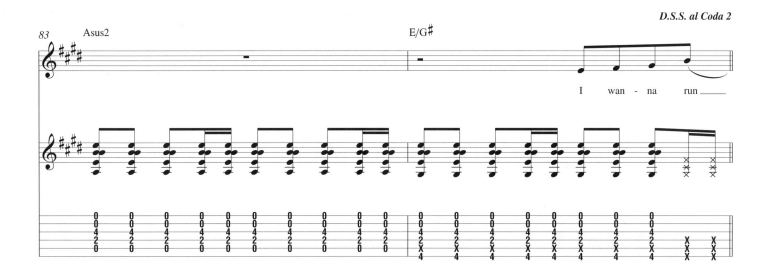

I wan - na run ____

Coda 2

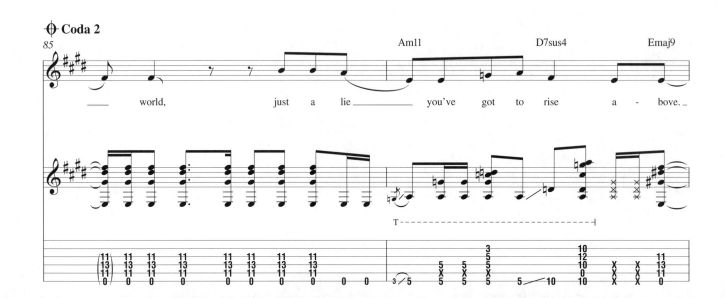

____ world, just a lie ____ you've got to rise a - bove. ____

Slow Dancing in a Burning Room
From *Continuum*, 2006

Following and revitalized by his 2005 Trio Tour, where guitar-centered blues was the reinvigorating focus of his musical efforts, John Mayer's third studio album benefits from the renewed guitar confidence he gained while rubbing shoulders with the approving likes of his blues heroes B.B. King, Buddy Guy, and Eric Clapton. Considered his finest album to date, the critically acclaimed *Continuum* boasts a veritable bevy of influences, styles, and solos that peppers the pop-rock song structure with passionate blues expression—now considered the signature of Mayer's style. "Slow Dancing in a Burning Room" is a perfect case in point. The verse–chorus structure fits the 3-1/2-minute, radio-friendly formula, but the extended blues solos and guitar textures outline this undeniable Mayer classic. For reference, the song transcription begins on page 26.

Intro
Built on a two-measure C#m, A–E chord progression that repeats the majority of the song, Mayer introduces the melodic hook with a solo guitar riff using mostly dyads. Played on his Custom Shop Black1 Strat with the middle pickup, the melodic hook is a descending scalar line from E to B, harmonized in 3rds and 4ths from the E major scale at the eighth/ninth position. Measure 2 shifts down to the fourth position for the A–E chord change. After restating the harmonized hook, he expands the chord vocabulary to a thumb-fretted Amaj9 chord.

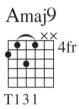

At measure 5, Gtr. 1 plays more Hendrix-style rhythm to make room for the entrance of the harmonized hook. This riffing is based out of the ninth-position C# minor pentatonic box.

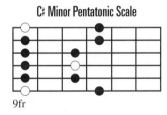

At measure 5, the melodic hook is enhanced by becoming a dual guitar affair, where the line is moved up an octave and harmonized in diatonic 3rds. Gtr. 2 plays the melody exclusively on the B string, while Gtr. 3 handles the 3rds harmony on the E string. This parallel motion of the two guitars allows them to maintain uniform articulations (i.e., bends, slides, and vibrato) for the hook's lyrical phrasing. If you take away the bends, here's how that phrase can be played by one guitar. In fact, John (or a second guitarist) often does something very similar to this when playing the song live.

Slow Dancing in a
Burning Room
Example 1

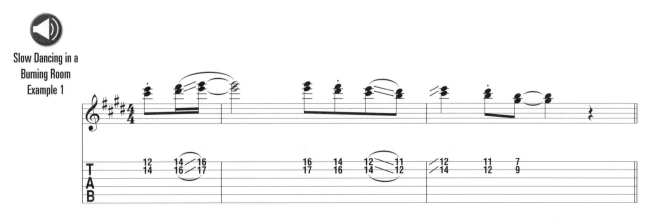

Verse

Gtr. 1 continues with the C#m-based riffing and fifth-position chording for a minimalist approach throughout the majority of the verse. In measure 15, he restates the harmonized hook in preparation for the uplifting mood of the chorus.

Serving as a constant for the deviations of Gtr. 1, Gtr. 4 enters and stutters its way through palm-muted C#m chords and strummed A6 chords, creating a motif that becomes a supporting texture throughout the song.

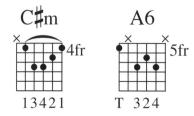

These chords may seem relatively basic, but the sequence of the top note of the voicings is significant. Despite their sparseness, the collective chords in this section successively follow a voice leading device of G# (5th of C#m), F# (6th of A6), and E (root) to create a descending line of subtle musical depth and attention.

Chorus

Gtr. 1 opts for laid-back, eighth- and 16th-note strumming for the six-measure chorus. It's composed of a pair of two-measure phrases (Badd4, C#m–A and Badd4, C#m–F#m11) articulated by fourth-string-root-based chords with a droning high E string (save for C#m). At measure 21, an acoustic (Gtr. 6) joins in with a supportive strumming part to add an extra layer of sonic interest.

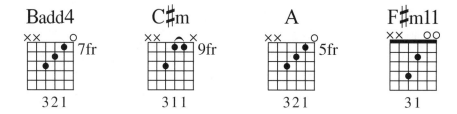

While the Badd4 and C#m chords are present in both phrases, the substitution of F#m11 for the A chord in the second phrase is no coincidence. F#m is the relative minor (6th) of A major, and because of that, they are often used interchangeably.

The entrance of Gtr. 5 introduces a repeating double-stop motif from measures 17–20 (**Riff B**). Hammering between D#/F# and E/G# dyads in 16th-note rhythm, they bring uplifting extensions to the B (13th and 11th), C#m (9th and 11th), A (maj7th, 13th, and #11th), and F#m chords (9th and 13th). This is par for the course when arranging textures for the chorus.

Guitar Solo

Here, John defaults to his truly blues phrasing over the repeating chord progression. Starting in the C# minor extension box, Mayer descends the scale with bluesy bends of varying degrees. This melodically simple phrase features whole and 1-1/2 step bends in similar rhythms. Measure 37 shifts things back to home base in ninth position for bends at the 11th fret of the G string before sliding into the 13th fret, dressing up the 3rd of E (G#) with a variety of vocal-like inflections. Use your ring finger for all the bending moves of this series.

Measure 38 continues with a bluesy, start-and-stop lick on the B and E strings and then fluidly descends the C# minor pentatonic scale with bends and pull-offs into measure 39, where he slides in and out of the extension box via 4th dyads. Use your ring and pinky fingers for the 4th shapes, rapidly moving your hand back and forth for the slides.

Bridge

Gtr. 5 returns with **Riff B**, introducing a whole new slew of extensions for a repeated, two-measure progression (F♯m–C♯m and B–F♯m).

Invoking the "crying" theme of the lyrics, Gtr. 9, pierced with a subtle octave effect, plays sustained bends to C♯, A, and G♯ for a longing texture of love's labors lost. Despite the position shifting from the 12th to ninth frets, he exclusively uses his ring finger for the bends. But to stay at the ninth position, it's possible to perform the half-step bends with your index and the whole-step bends with your ring finger, so use whichever is more comfortable.

Outro

The outro brings everything back and then some. Atop the strumming of **Rhy. Fig. 2**, the harmonized intro riff, and the mournful vocal reminder of "Burning Room," Mayer painfully ushers forth melodic blues licks practically devoid of cliché. In measures 49–50, he plays around the holes, drawing exclusively from the ninth-position C♯ minor pentatonic, making room for the restatement of the harmonized intro. The picking in measure 50 can be tricky, so I'd advise employing a concept called *economy picking*, in which you follow an upstroke or downstroke with the same when crossing to neighboring strings.

Slow Dancing in a
Burning Room
Example 2

However, that's where the pretense ends and the unbridled emotional turmoil erupts from his fingers through fluid technical flurries and angst-ridden bends. Highlights include homages to Albert King (measures 52–53), Jimmy Page-inspired repeating licks (measures 55–56), and 32nd-note legato lines (measure 57), so turn up the volume on your speakers to hear the passionate fluidity of these lines as the song fades.

SLOW DANCING IN A BURNING ROOM

Words and Music by John Mayer

Slow Dancing in a
Burning Room
Full Song

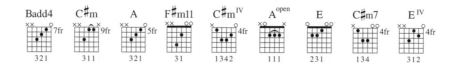

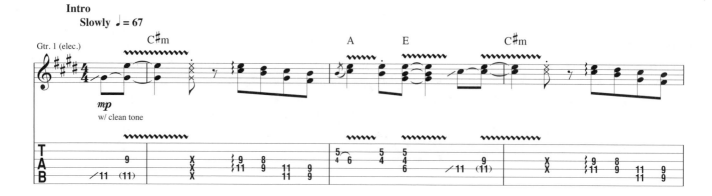

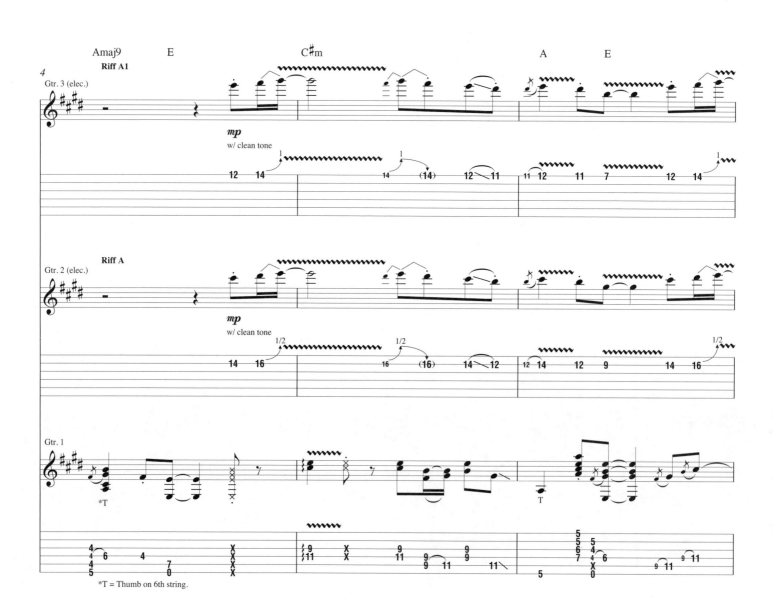

*T = Thumb on 6th string.

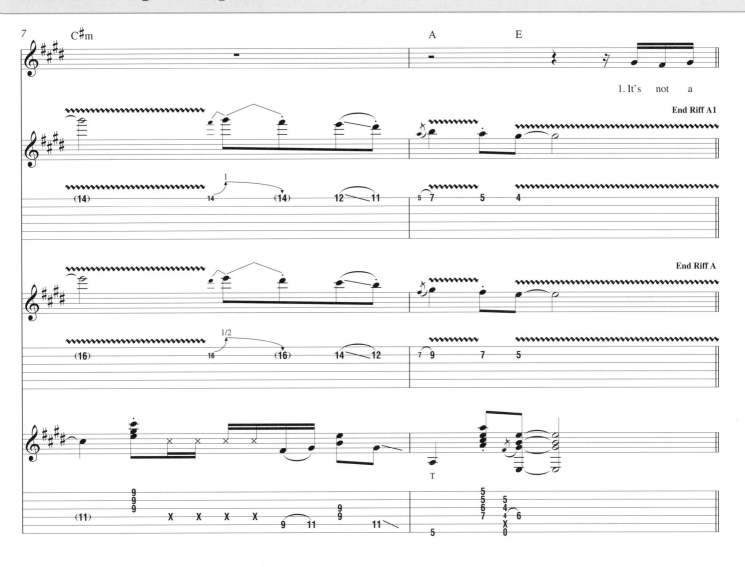

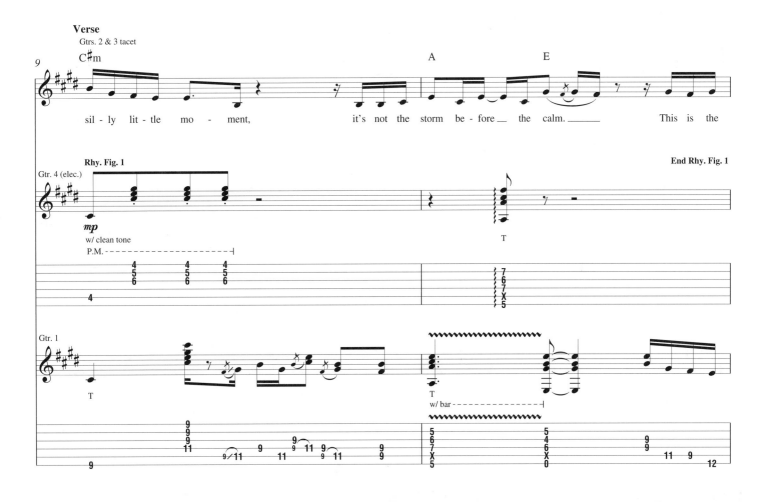

Verse

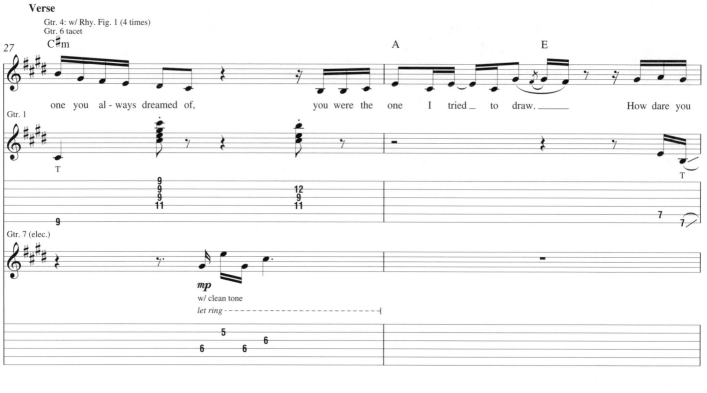

hit me just to hurt me so you leave me feel - ing dir - ty 'cause you can't un - der - stand. We're go - ing

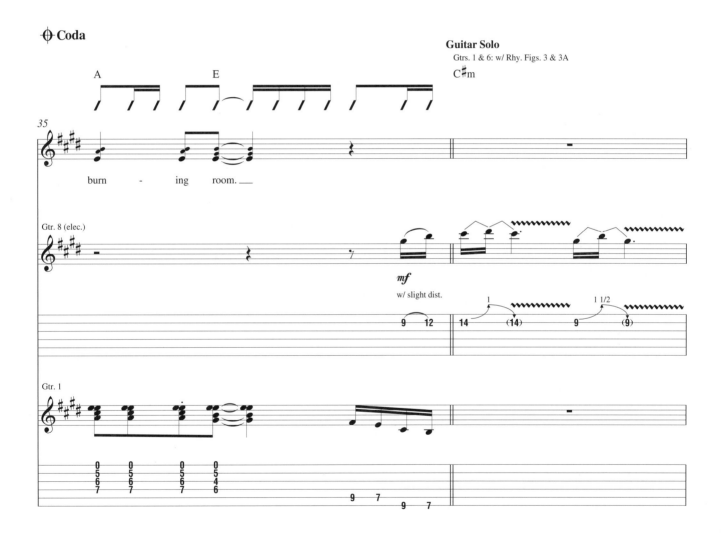

burn - ing room. ___

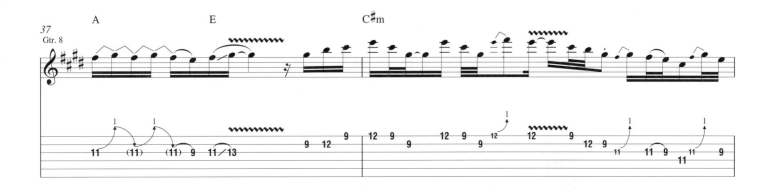

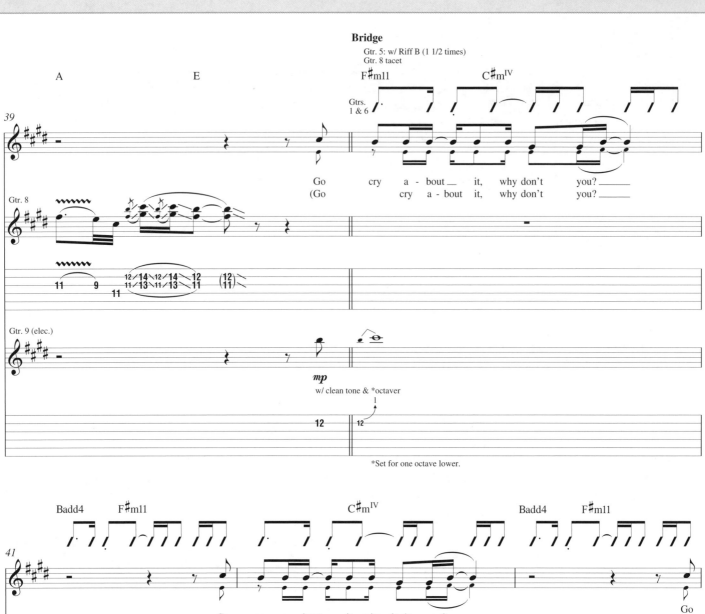

*Set for one octave lower.

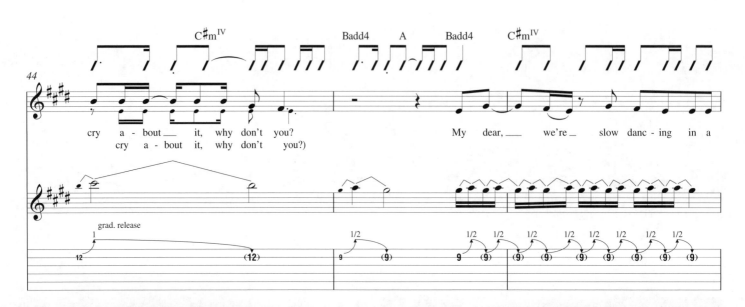

Outro
Gtrs. 1 & 6: w/ Rhy. Fig. 2 (till end)
Gtr. 9 tacet

*Refers to downstemmed notes only.

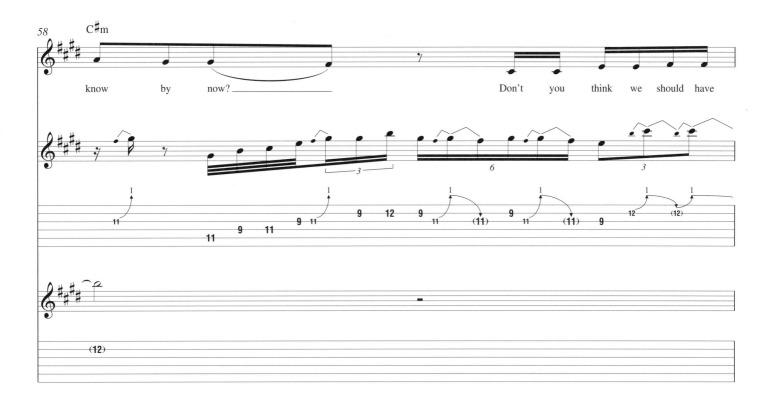

know by now? _____ Don't you think we should have

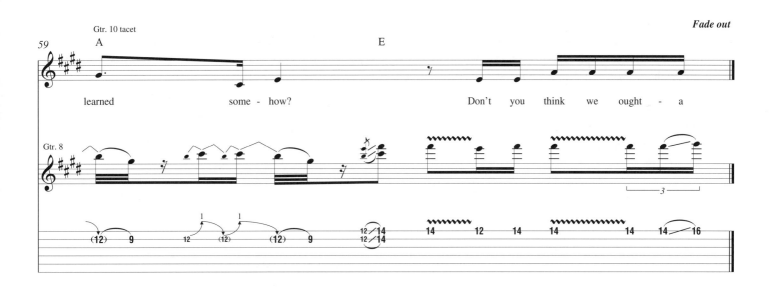

learned some - how? Don't you think we ought - a

Bold as Love
From *Continuum*, 2006

While Hendrix and SRV covers have been mainstays of John's live concerts and single releases since 2001, "Bold as Love" is a first for Mayer because of its inclusion on the Grammy Award-winning *Continuum*. Where most artists wouldn't dare tread the hallowed grounds of the legend's repertoire, Mayer brazenly assaults us with an updated interpretation of the Hendrix classic that stays true to the original and firmly establishes John as a bona fide bluesman with performance guts, musical intensity, and soloing artistry. For reference, the song transcription begins on page 40.

Like the almighty Jimi Hendrix recording, John tunes his guitar down a half step for this song. To get in the same key as the recording, here's what you do: match the 12th-fret harmonic of the low E with the sixth fret of the A string (E♭), then tune the rest of the guitar relative to that E♭.

Verse

The verse is a looped A–E–F♯m–D progression with a D–C♯m change towards a harmonically stimulating transition to the pre-chorus. Here are the primary grips John uses to negotiate the changes.

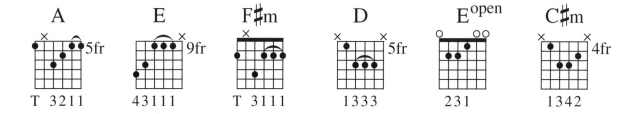

With these forms, his rhythmic treatment alternates by playing the root and adding fills based on the chords. These are primarily drawn from their respective pentatonic shapes and allow you to keep holding the chord form as you hammer these extra notes with your ring or pinky fingers. The sixth-string-root chords, be it major or minor, use the same embellishments on the G and E strings for color (4th and 2nd, respectively).

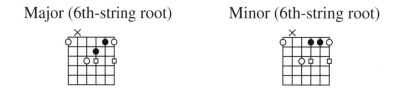

Major (6th-string root)   Minor (6th-string root)

The fifth-string-root shape climbs the neck for a comfortable ring–index fingering. Where the sixth-string root sees both major and minor qualities, this shape is only applied to the E and D major chords of the verse.

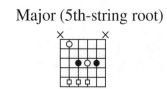

Major (5th-string root)

This style of rhythm playing is reverently referred to as "Hendrix rhythm" because of Jimi's hybrid lead/rhythm method of accompaniment. Blurring the lines of melody and pulse is how Hendrix's contribution to our sonic lexicon lives on in the well-learned hands of John Mayer.

Where measure 8 was previously a D chord (the last measure of the four-bar progression), he breaks up the cycle by adding a C♯m chord on beat 3. This is a useful addition because the pre-chorus starts on a D chord and, to avoid an uneventful transition, he creates variety with a half-step resolution, serving the larger structure of the song.

Pre-Chorus

The pre-chorus consists of a looped D, A, Bm, G progression with the necessary Hendrix-style rhythm, adding interesting fill variations. While the majority of the riffing uses concepts from the verse, measures 12 and 14 expound on the ideas of the sixth-string-root shapes. The fills for the G chord are based in the second position, where your index and middle fingers grab the G and B strings as the ring finger hammers into the 3rd of G (B on the fourth fret, G string). Reaching for the fifth fret, D string with the pinky while holding the shape is a bit of a stretch, so practice that move relaxed and slowly at first.

G

Measure 14 has a nice, 6th-interval walkup in eighth notes. To keep your hand in position, use your ring and pinky fingers for the G and E strings, respectively, and then move your hand to shift the shape up to the ninth fret and back.

Major 6th shapes (6th-string root)

Measure 16 calls upon a device similar to the one used in measure 8, in which he adds a chromatic passing chord on beat 3 to close the section. This time, it moves up to G♯, moving toward the A chord that opens the chorus.

More Than Meets the Eye
The structure of the verse and pre-chorus progressions is no coincidence. When you take a look at each, side by side, the similarities between the two become obvious, and their disguised simplicity is genius.

The verse is an A–E–F♯m–D progression (dashes are used to show it as a complete unit). Relative to the key of A (the key of the song), these chords are harmonically analyzed as I–V–vi–IV (because if you count up from A, you'll get these numbers). This is a common progression in rock.

Now, the pre-chorus has a D–A–Bm–G progression. Relative to the key of A, the chords are IV–I–ii–♭VII. Thinking from this point of view, the ♭VII chord is a *borrowed chord* (meaning it's "borrowed" from the parallel key of A minor). But if you analyze the progression relative to the D chord (the chord that starts the progression), you get I–V–vi–IV—the very same analysis as the verse progression!

The verse and pre-chorus are intervallic copies of each other, where the verse is relative to the A chord (I chord) and the pre-chorus is relative to the D chord (IV chord). With this, we've now discovered a powerful songwriting concept: the same progression based on the I chord can be used for the IV chord. This interplay of the I and IV chord is all over music and happens as well in the chorus of "Perfectly Lonely." Check out the analysis for the chorus on page 53 to discover other fascinating ways these chords can work together.

Chorus

Gtr. 1 abandons the choppy Hendrix rhythms in favor of strumming full, tight chords. This changes the mood from bouncy to a sparkly, uplifting feel, which is heightened even more when he adds the sliding 6th dyads. He starts in fifth position for the A and E7 chords and then hovers around the second and third positions for the F♯m and G chords, respectively.

In measure 23, he arpeggiates an interesting Dadd9 voicing in quarter-note triplets. Fret the F♯ on fret 9 with your pinky while you barre the fifth fret. Hold down the whole shape as you let the notes ring together with the suggested fingering.

Dadd2

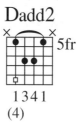

1 3 4 1
(4)

Interlude

At measure 28, he returns to the root-fill style of the verse. Because his singing duties are paused for the moment, he aggressively hammers through the seventh-position B minor pentatonic scale in measure 30. For this, barre the seventh-fret double stops with your index as your ring finger handles the ninth-fret acrobatics. After you grab the ninth-fret slide on the A and D strings with your ring and pinky fingers, respectively, slide to the fifth fret of the A string with your index for the familiar pentatonic walkups.

Guitar Solo

Occurring over the looped chorus progression, Mayer's solo pays homage to Hendrix by boasting a veritable host of aggressive licks. He starts with call-and-response lines rooted in the second-position A major pentatonic scale.

A Major Pentatonic Scale
(F♯ Minor Pentatonic Scale)

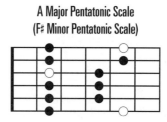

Here, he carefully addresses the chord tones before momentarily sliding up to the fifth position with A and E major arpeggio spellings, graced with vibrato-laden bends. He then reverts back to the second-position F♯ minor pentatonic for a legato line in smooth triplets before climbing the neck with sliding 6th and 3rd shapes, landing on the 10th-position B.B. box in A.

B.B. Box (Key of A)

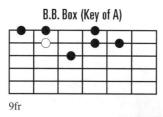

9fr

Here, he milks the box for all its worth with a well-constructed variety of repeating licks. He plays a series of bends as a changing rhythmic and obstinate harmonic motif. Over the A chord, he bends the 12th-fret B on string 2 a whole step with his ring finger, alternating it with the 10th-fret D note of the E string held by his index. He repeats this move before speeding up the two-note lick to a triplet rhythm, where the bending accents move to different places on the beat as a result. He continues this for the next two measures with a slight change: the ring finger bends the 13th fret, creating a unison bend (see photo) with the 10th-fret D note on string 1, where it serves unique functions over the E7 (♭7th) and F♯m7 (♭6th) chords. Be sure to practice keeping the notes from ringing into one another, as the separation is vital for the line's rhythmic quality.

He anticipates the G chord change in measure 76 with a huge double-stop bend of 1-1/2 steps and then races down the A minor pentatonic scale, creating a bend/descent motif he'll use over the next four measures. Use an upstroke (∨) for the E–B string crossing after the bend/releases to maintain the legato feel of this speedy line.

For the double-stop bends, the extremity of the bend is best performed by catching the B string under your bending finger as you stretch the E string. This is a tricky maneuver, as it depends on where your finger comes in contact with the string, so allow the edge of the fingertip to cover the adjacent string. Check out the Stevie Ray Vaughan section of the Essential Licks chapter for a detailed explanation of this technique at work (page 84).

The third and final ascent of the solo brings us all the way up to the 17th-position A major pentatonic, where he plucks the high root note (A) on the E string in laid-back triplets while shaking the heck out of the strings. He then uses this note as home base for a bluesy display of bends on increasing frets. The final four measures of the solo feature identical double-stop phrases at the 17th and fifth positions. It's all out of A major pentatonic, so your index and ring fingers take care of the 17th/fifth and 19th/seventh frets, respectively. For the double-stop hammer-ons on beat 3 of measures 85 and 86, you have to momentarily switch positions to cleanly grab the 16th/fourth fret with your index, while your middle takes care of the 17th/fifth fret (similar to the G double-stop fills heard in the pre-chorus). He then closes the solo with a slick second-position eighth-note/triplet phrase over F♯m, reminiscent of the solo's opening statements (measure 71).

Breakdown

The breakdown quiets the proceedings, delaying the final chorus with an interplay of delicate fills and mellow rhythms from Gtrs. 3 and 1, respectively. Played over an extended version of the verse progression, Gtr. 3 rolls off the volume, cleaning up the overdriven tone for B.B. King-style subtlety over the rounded warmth of Gtr. 1's neck pickup. With a reduced version of Hendrix rhythm as a sonic backdrop, Gtr. 3's fill vocabulary mixes octave slides, fifth-position minor pentatonic pull-offs, and 12th-fret pre-bends on the B string.

At measure 105, Mayer restricts himself to fifth-position A major/minor pentatonics for the remainder of the breakdown. Here, he gradually develops double-stop triplet ideas of increasing complexity. Over the A and E chords, he repeats a descending 4ths/pull-off figure with double stops in between. For the descending 4ths on beats 1 and 2, use finger rolling to cross the strings and then an index-finger barre for the hammered double stops; be quick with your position shifts to reach the 16th-note triplets in time.

To signal the *crescendo* (band gets louder), Gtr. 3 plays a four-note double-stop pattern in triplets. Barre the fifth fret with your index finger and hammer on the sixth fret with your middle. Then play the seventh fret of the D string with your ring (this note is used as a pivot point). For the seventh-fret double stop, simply collapse your ring finger at the joint for the barre.

Outro-Chorus

Propelled by the motion of the breakdown, the outro-chorus *modulates* to the key of C. This change of key adds lift and dynamics to the proceedings because we've been primarily playing a four-chord loop in A for the entire song. Gtrs. 1 and 2 transpose the sixth-string-root chords and 6th shapes up three frets to the eighth position, while Gtr. 4 offers similar sus2- and minor-based double-stop figures on strings 4–2.

Measure 124 closes the song with a classic Hendrix hook that consists of a hammered 10th-position F/A chord played in quarter-note triplets, which is followed by a full-blown C chord at the eighth fret. For the F/A chord, barre strings 5–3 with your index at the 10th fret and hammer the 12th fret with your ring finger as you close this great Hendrix cover with confidence.

Bold as Love
Full Song

BOLD AS LOVE
Words and Music by Jimi Hendrix

Tune down 1/2 step:
(low to high) E♭-A♭-D♭-G♭-B♭-E♭

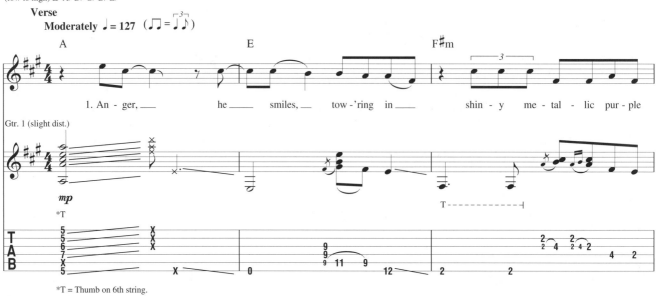

*T = Thumb on 6th string.

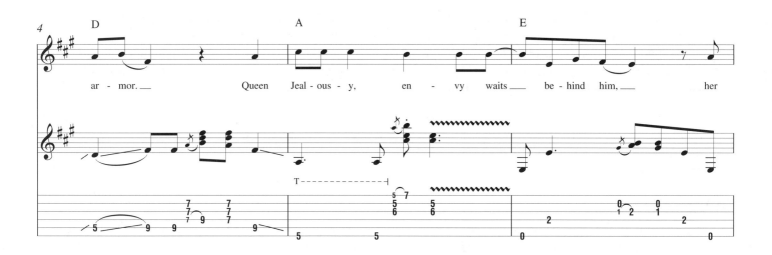

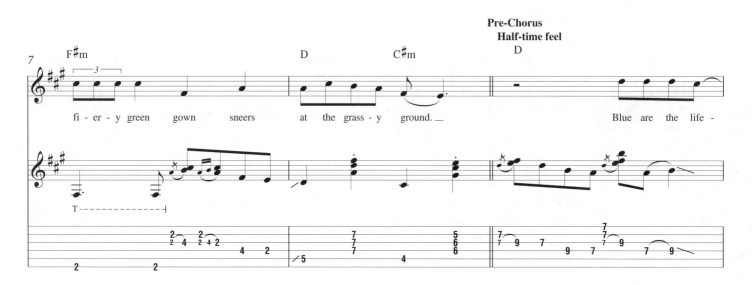

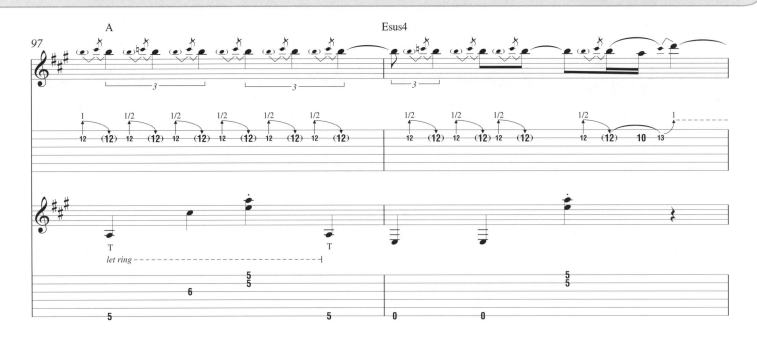

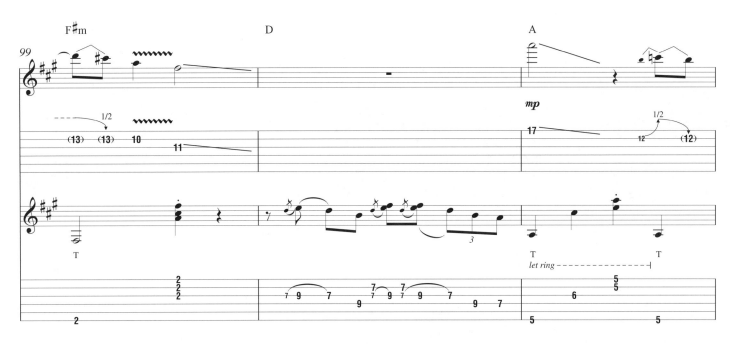

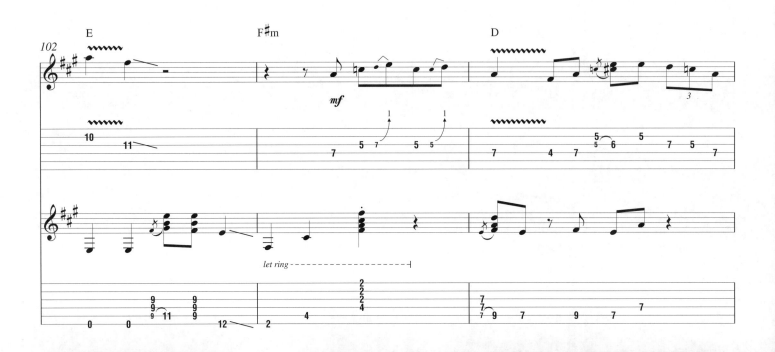

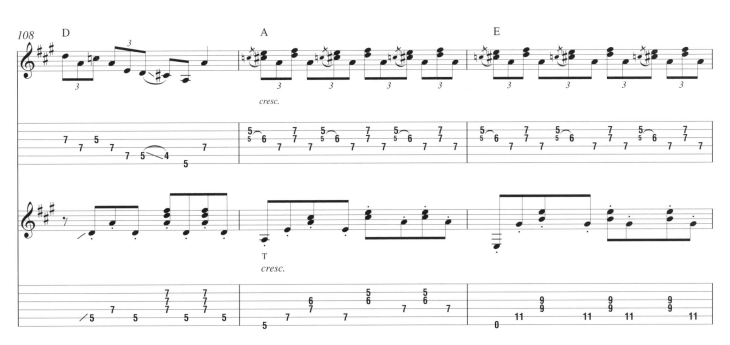

Outro-Chorus

Gtr. 3 tacet

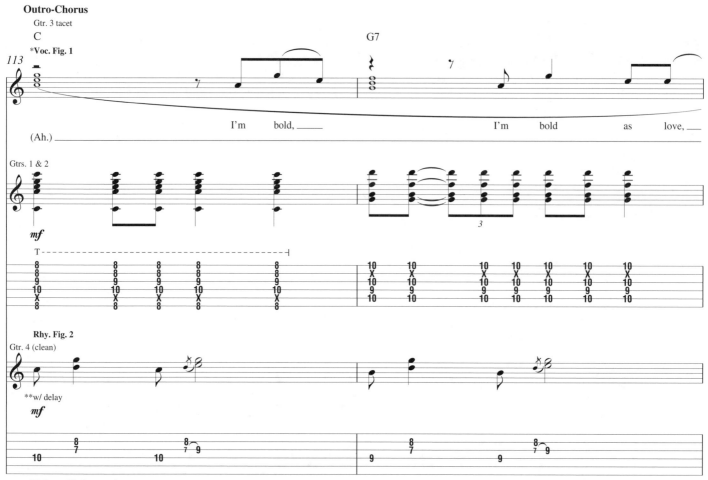

*Refers to bkgd. voc. only.

**Set to quarter-note-triplet regeneration.

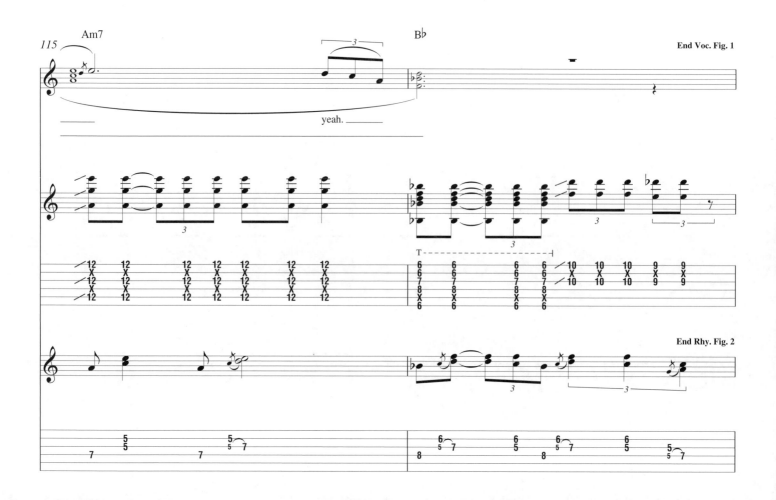

Perfectly Lonely
From *Battle Studies*, 2009

In 2009, John once again found himself continuing to be creatively eclectic. Having treaded the waters of acoustic, electric, pop, and blues in his previous releases, John's fourth studio release, *Battle Studies*, focuses on the California side of his influences with the songwriting stamps of Tom Petty, the Eagles, and Fleetwood Mac. Born out of an intensive writing schedule that lasted over six months, the 11-track album went on to garner critical acclaim and multiple Grammy Award nominations.

Among those tracks was the fourth single, "Perfectly Lonely." Written as a rationalization for being seemingly content with his single status, John later admitted that it's a "3-1/2 minute lie." The Tom Petty simplicity of the looping chord progression with the subtle songcraft and melodic soloing that Mayer brings to the table makes this a fun, easy rocker. For reference, the song transcription begins on page 56.

Intro

The majority of the song is based on a four-measure C–F–Dm–G progression with an "and" of beat 4 anticipation every other measure. Gtrs. 1 and 2 rely on position-shifting chord shapes with subtle fills throughout. Measure 1 opens with a fifth-string-root C chord followed by a two-beat walkup through the major pentatonic scale. Here's the chord shape with highlighted embellishments.

With an eighth-note anticipation into measure 2, he quickly moves back to the first position for the F major barre chord. After three syncopated strums, he uses his ring finger to barre an accented C/G chord on the "ee" of beat 4 (second 16th note of the beat in a "1-ee-and-uh" counting scheme) in preparation for moving towards the 10th-position Dm chord. The four-bar progression ends at the third-position G chord. This repeats for 90 percent of the song, so it's excellent practice for position shifts and thumb-fretting accuracy.

Gtr. 3's pedal steel-inspired intro hook punctuates the groove with sliding 4ths, plucked 6ths, and hammered 3rd intervals derived from the C major scale. Measures 1 and 3 similarly open with descending dyads and end on the "and" of beat 4 with hammered 3rds to match the F and G chords. For the F chord, he addresses the 3rd/5th dyad (A/C; 14th/13th frets) with an index–ring hammer-on while the middle finger frets the B string. The G chord has a top-note hammer-on with an index–pinky slur to the 3rd (B) while the ring finger holds the root.

Measure 5 continues with B.B.-inspired major pentatonics at the 13th position in C. Here's the complete B.B. box from which Mayer undoubtedly draws his lines.

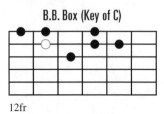

Here, he dances back and forth between the A and C notes (14th fret, G string and 13th fret, B string), most likely fingerpicked with the thumb and middle finger. He continues with a *minor 2nd* oblique bend, where the bent note is a half step away from the fretted note, for a pedal steel-style articulation. He then shifts down to an eighth-position G blues line in preparation for the G chord. The seamless position-shifting continues for another oblique bend at the

20th fret of both the B and E strings. Keep your pinky firmly planted on the E string as you bend the B string with your ring finger, allowing both notes to ring together. The difficulty is staying in tune for the isolated bending motion, so check the fretted equivalents if you feel you're off.

Verse 1 & Pre-Chorus 1

Gtr. 3 takes its leave as the vocals enter, and Gtrs. 1 and 2 continue their rhythmic duties with subtle fills on the Dm and G chords, where the pinky takes an active role on the G string for both chords at their respective positions. At measure 11, he addresses the 5th for a Dm walkdown and at measure 12 momentarily hints at a Gsus4 accent on the "and" of beat 4. Measures 15–24 follow in similar suit, but more aggressive hammer-ons for the Dm and Gsus4 chords build intensity to the chorus.

Chorus

The C–F–Dm–G progression continues through the chorus but sees a three-measure variation of Em7–Am–Dm7–G, starting at measure 29. Em7 and Am are both sixth-string roots, and the fifth-position Dm7 chord makes for a more compact sequence as far as chord-switching is concerned.

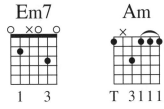

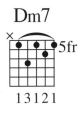

Chord Talk

Similar to the songwriting concepts in "Bold as Love" (see pre-chorus analysis on page 37), the variations of the C–F–Dm–G and Em7–Am–Dm7–G are related. While the last two chords are obviously identical, the connection between the C–F (I–IV) and Em7–Am (iii–vi) chords is the one with which we'll concern ourselves. If we isolate each pair, the C–Em7 (I–iii) and F–Am (IV–vi) chords are a 3rd interval away from each other. This is known as *tertial harmony*, where chords built from a 3rd above the root have a related harmonic function. The fact that the new chords are minor relies on the key we're in, but the more important thing is which chords are being changed.

Once again, we see that the same alterations are being applied to both the I and IV chords. These chords' importance to western harmony is the basis of how we've been conditioned to hear music, and they're the backbone for most progressions. So, keep an eye out for your chances to use these concepts when you're building your own progressions.

Verse 2 & Pre-Chorus 2

While Gtrs. 1 and 2 retain the comping ideas of the initial verse, Gtr. 3 makes a 16-measure appearance for the second verse and pre-chorus. With subtle 6ths and top-string triple stops, he fills around the vocals for an airy R&B feel.

With the vocals particularly active, Gtr. 3 places fills on beats 2–4 of every other measure, landing on both F and G chords. The F fills in measures 38 and 42 are derived from the fifth-position major pentatonic shape in hammer-chord form and single-note lines, respectively.

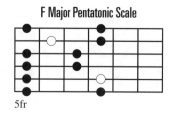

The fluid, sliding 6ths fill over the G chord of measure 44 caps verse 2. For the notes on parallel frets, use your ring and pinky fingers for the G and E strings (low to high) and grab the fourth fret with your middle finger while your index takes care of the third fret, bringing you back to home base.

Pre-chorus 2 keeps the wide-interval motif as a more spacious texture on the A and G strings. He doesn't exclusively use the 6ths, but he mainly targets chord tones with smooth voice leading that yield interesting intervals like 5ths and octaves, as well.

Where pre-chorus 1 used the looping C–F–Dm–G progression, he alters this progression in the same manner as the chorus (with tertial harmony) to restate the Em–Am–Dm7–G chord sequence.

Bridge

The bridge brings new harmonic rhythm to the song with an Am–C/E–F–G–Gsus4 progression. The Am and C/E chords are both fifth-position voicings that use the same pentatonic fill in their respective measures.

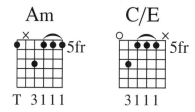

The F and G changes use a root–chord strumming pattern in eighth notes that skips the fifth strum of each measure. For the G chord, follow a down–up–down–up–up–up pattern with the Gsus4 change on the "ee" of beat 4.

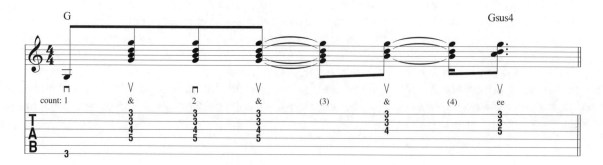

The Am–C/E–F cycles through once more but adds one new chord and another songwriting concept to the party. To play the Fm chord in measure 61, simply lift your middle finger from the second fret of the F chord while barring fret 1.

Since we've been using the V chord (G chord) to get back to the I (C) all day long, he uses Fm to lift towards the guitar solo. Fm, functioning as a iv chord, is found in classical harmony as a way to resolve to the I chord with unique tension. Why does it work? Well, Fm and C share a common tone, and the rest are separated by a half step. If you look at each triad, you'll see that Fm is composed of F–A♭–C notes, while a C triad has C–E–G notes.

Similar to the G chord in the pre-chorus of "Bold as Love" (see page 37), this is a borrowed chord—in this case, it's borrowed from the parallel key of C minor. Study the following example, keeping in mind that the first note of each pair is from the Fm chord and the second is from C. You'll see that F–E and A♭–G notes both resolve by a half step, while the C note is a common tone of each chord.

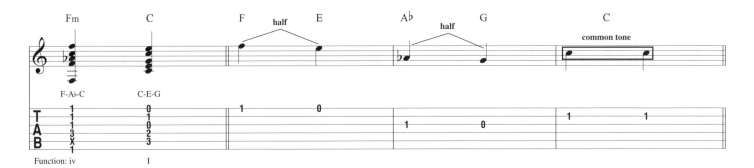

Guitar Solo

This simple guitar solo is full of melodic contour, articulation subtlety, and scale variety. In measures 61–63, he draws primarily from the fifth-position C major pentatonic, disguising his usage with how he slides to the same note to which he bent. In the next example, check out how his initial thoughts directly quote the melody of the vocal line.

Perfectly Lonely
Example 1

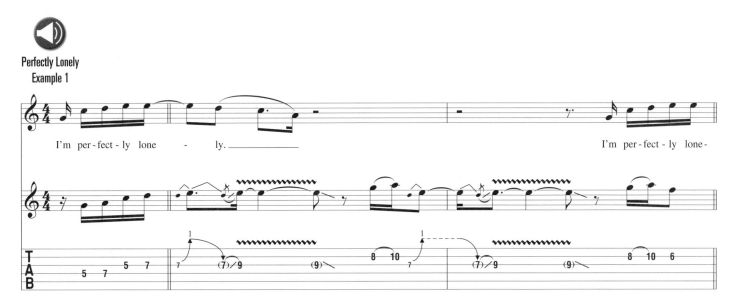

The remainder of his time at the fifth position is spent with other sliding innovations. In measure 64, instead of simply fretting notes as he descends the scale, he approaches most of the scale tones from a whole step above with a grace-note slide. He then smoothly ascends the neck for the second half of the eight-bar solo.

After a two-fold, whole-step bend at the 11th fret on the B string, he yet again shifts to the 13th-position B.B. box in C for a unison bend/pull-off blues lick. He repeats this and then continues with an anticipating series of bend/vibrato moves on the 15th fret, E string, and finishes with a stellar bend-slide maneuver to the 20th fret, clad with generous amounts of vibrato.

Outro

The outro builds with a repeating background vocal and a sparring lick competition between Gtrs. 3 and 6. Where Gtr. 3 plays half of the intro hook and then fills around the rest, Gtr. 6 negotiates the holes with bends at the 15th fret, E string. At measure 75, Gtr. 6 lets Gtr. 3 struggle through a series of bend-and-releases that go higher until two whole steps are painfully coaxed out of the strings. Then at measure 80, Gtr. 6 rejoins with impressive 16th-note legato lines, replete with a variety of bends. Gtr. 3 responds to that with lyrical bends and flawless position shifting, as the guitar duel continues to the fade.

Perfectly Lonely Full Song

PERFECTLY LONELY
Words and Music by John Mayer

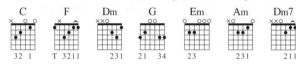

Intro
Moderately ♩ = 92

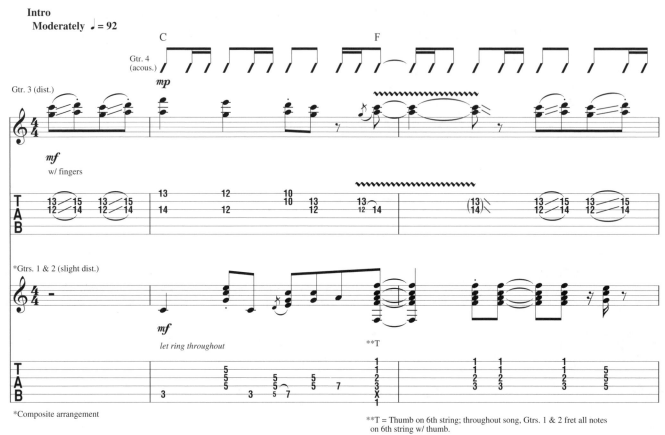

*Composite arrangement

**T = Thumb on 6th string; throughout song, Gtrs. 1 & 2 fret all notes on 6th string w/ thumb.

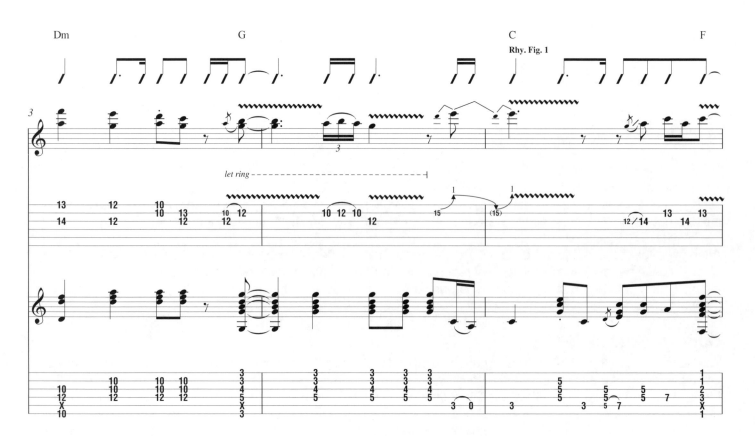

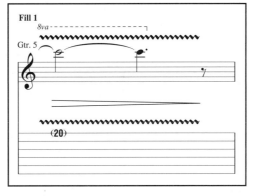

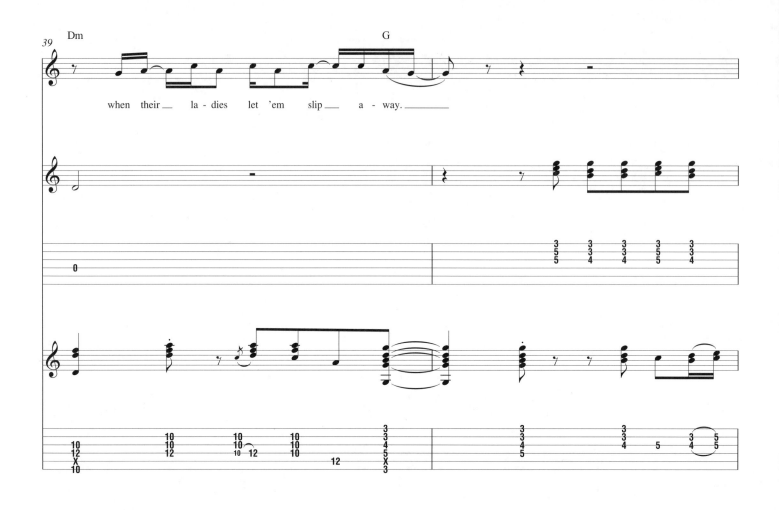

when their __ la - dies let 'em slip __ a - way. __

And when they ask __ me how I'm do - in' with mine,

Pre-Chorus

Gtr. 4: w/ Rhy. Fig. 2

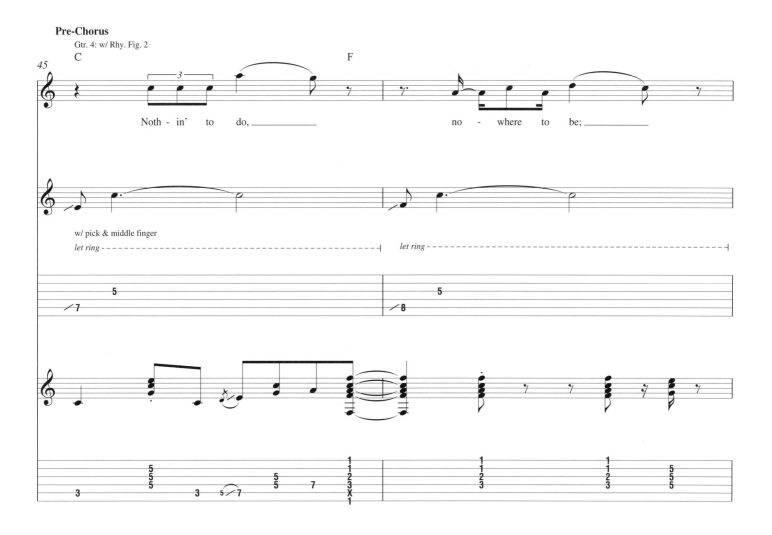

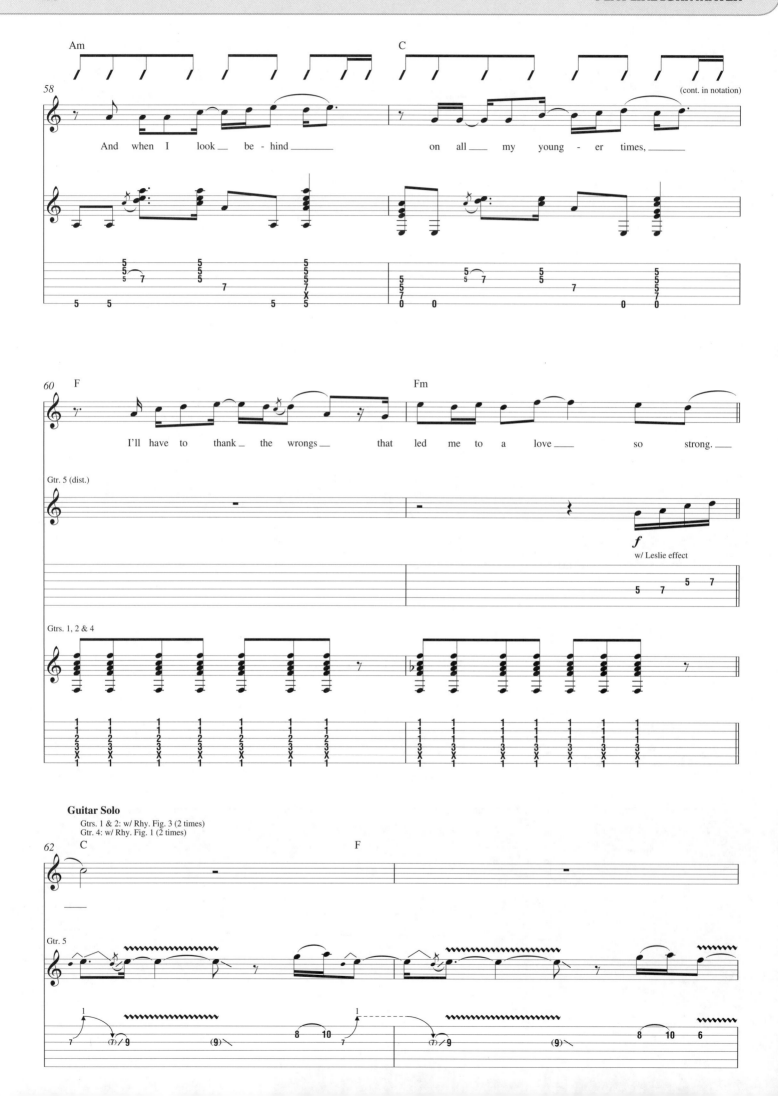

And when I look be-hind on all my young - er times,

I'll have to thank the wrongs that led me to a love so strong.

Gtr. 5 (dist.)

f
w/ Leslie effect

Gtrs. 1, 2 & 4

Guitar Solo
Gtrs. 1 & 2: w/ Rhy. Fig. 3 (2 times)
Gtr. 4: w/ Rhy. Fig. 1 (2 times)

Gtr. 5

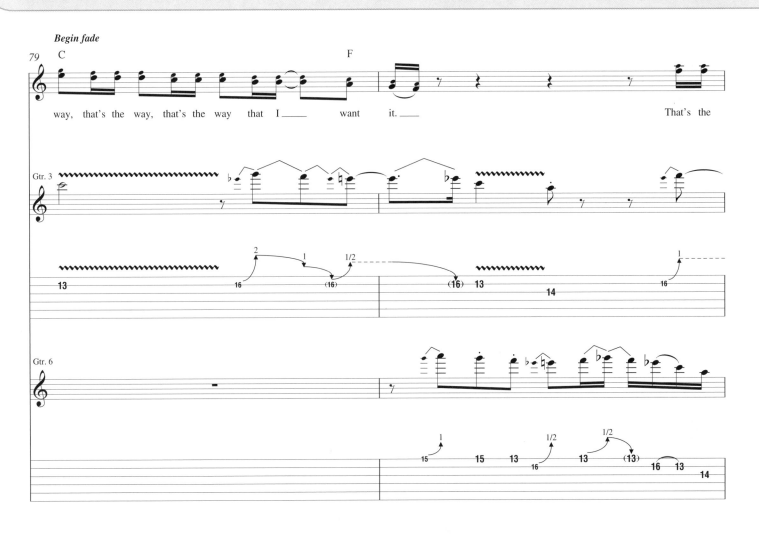

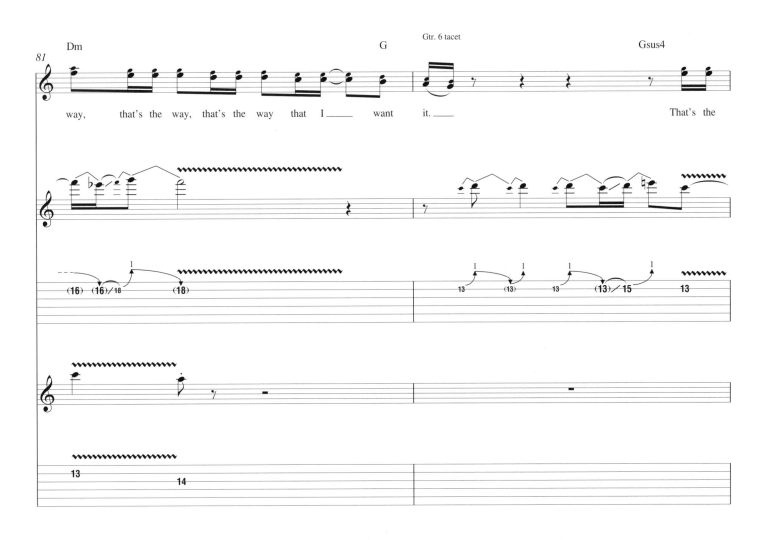

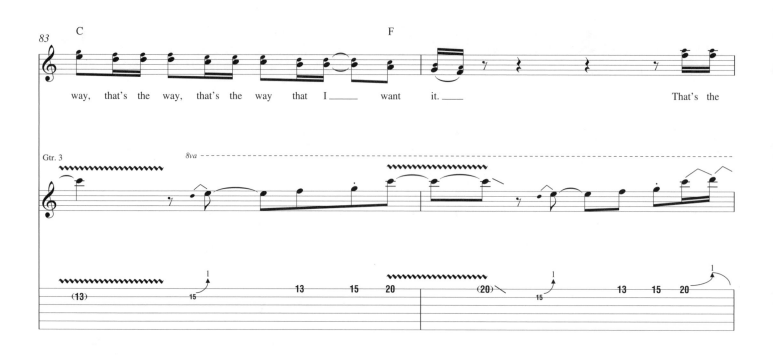

way, that's the way, that's the way that I _____ want it. _____   That's the

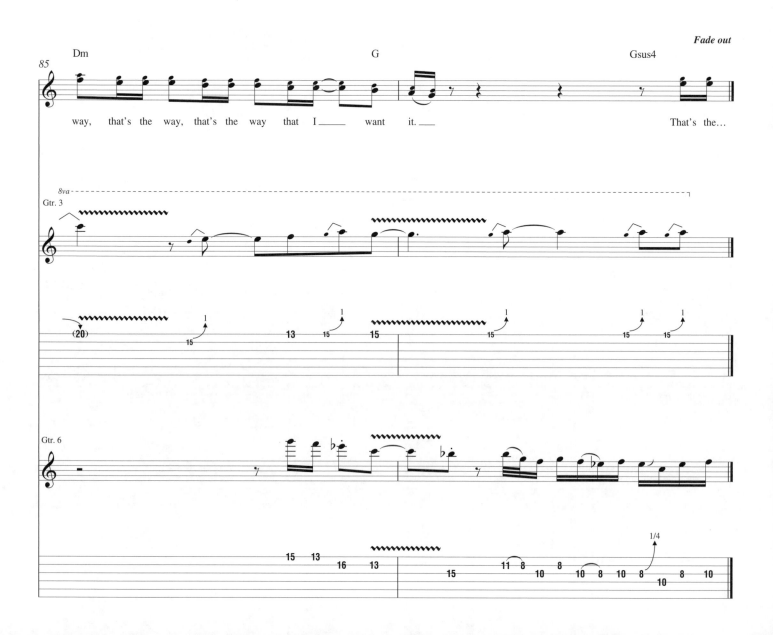

way, that's the way, that's the way that I _____ want it. _____   That's the...

Gravity
From *Continuum*, 2006

Penned as a "reminder to stay on the noble path" for Mayer's chart-topping studio album *Continuum*, "Gravity" is an intimately somber major blues with the weight of the world on its shoulders. John's delicate fills and soaring, lyrical soloing are at their most dynamic, leaving musical space for the central theme of "the most important song [he's] ever written." Check out the transcription on page 75 to learn why "Gravity" became #84 on *Rolling Stone*'s list of the 100 Greatest Guitar Songs of All Time.

Intro

With his Custom Shop Black1 Strat on the neck pickup, John invokes the main theme with B.B.-style expression and simplicity. Starting with a delicate slide, Gtr. 2 stutter-plucks and bends up the G major pentatonic scale from the 6th (E), through the root (G), and to the 3rd (B), adding a bit of quivering vibrato to the whole-step bend.

Gravity
Example 1

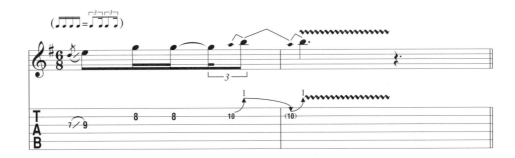

John's rhythmic treatment of his careful note choices adds to the beauty of the intro. His languid phrasing almost suggests that he doesn't know where the subdivisions lie, but this is a deliberately subtle indicator of his blues influence. The art of laying back or rushing your phrases before finally landing squarely on the beat is an oft-underused skill in manipulating your listener's sense of tension and release. As you can hear, Mayer expertly applies this technique and eventually finds his rhythmic footing on beat 1, measure 3 with an unarticulated bend.

John uses this five-note motif, with dragged rhythm intact, as an integral part of his phrasing structure for the intro. Entering on beat 4 and ending near beat 1, he modifies the last notes of the phrase to fit the chord on which he lands, often adding special tensions. For the C chord in measure 5, he bends to the B and follows quickly with the A (6th of C, 10th fret). In measure 7, he holds the bend, and in measure 9, he releases the bend and hits the G note (5th of C, eighth fret). All because of his repeated use of the motif as a harmonic anchor, the few note changes made garner a lot of musical mileage—the essence of lyrical blues phrasing.

In support of this delicate lick, Gtr. 1 sparsely comps the eight-measure, G–C intro and plays sustained voicings with double-stop fills in between. The G chord is a standard sixth-string root, but he commonly hammers into a B/D dyad in the second measure of the chord. It starts with a D5 chord shape, but play the third fret with your middle finger instead so your ring can hammer on to the fourth fret. Here's the G chord with highlighted color tones from which he builds his fills.

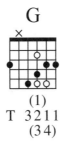

G

The C voicing is an interesting, fifth-position chord with an E as the root. Because the bass is playing a C at this time, the chord symbol doesn't reflect this inversion, but let's refer to this shape as C/E.

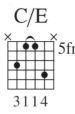

Because of its location, it conveniently lends itself to fifth-position C major pentatonic fills and G major scale double stops. Play the double stops with a ring/index finger form, sliding the shape up to the 9/7 dyad on the D and G strings, while keeping the C/E chord as your focal point.

Verse

As Mayer's intimate vocal delivery takes center stage, Gtr. 1 follows the same musical courtesy of the intro by playing around the vocals with double stops and descending lines throughout the verse.

While holding the third fret, E string with his thumb, he plays 3rd dyads on the G and B strings towards the tail-end of measure 11. For the pair of notes on the fifth fret, use your ring and pinky fingers to individually fret the notes so they ring clearly. At measure 14, he merely implies the C chord change with a slow, double-stop riff from C major pentatonic that smoothly slides back to the third-position G chord.

To close out the last four measures of the verse, he plays 6th intervals, with D as a common tone, to hammered double stops from C major pentatonic, creating forward motion to the chorus.

Chorus

The chorus is composed of an eight-measure progression where unique grips of Am7 and D7 get two measures each, followed by a Gm/B♭–E♭maj7 turnaround, chromatically resolving to D7. He arpeggiates through each of these in a similar rhythm to highlight their harmonically disparate voice-leading qualities, as they smoothly move from one chord to the next.

For Am7, simply move your ring finger to the seventh fret, D string from the C/E chord.

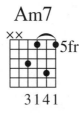

D7 is an uncommon voicing, built from a root–3rd–♭7th–3rd formula (low to high). The 3rd intervals on both the D and B strings create a complex voicing by setting the *tritone interval* (3rd and ♭7th) next to each other, making the challenging stretch worthwhile. The alternate D7, by contrast, is a more commonplace choice, so strum through both.

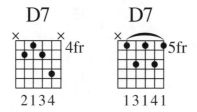

The Gm/B♭ and E♭maj7 chords are obviously foreign to the pop context of a G major song, so familiarize yourself with the grips before we uncover their purpose.

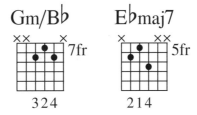

Thinking Out Loud

While the chorus progression starts with an Am7–D7 progression (iim7–V7 in G), the next changes of Gm/B♭–E♭maj7 resolve to D7 in a unique way. First, let's simplify their harmony by stripping away the voice leading elements, because the extensions (e.g., maj7) and the alternate bass notes (e.g., B♭) don't have an effect on their musical function within the song. So by changing Gm/B♭ to Gm, E♭maj7 to E♭, and D7 to D, we now have an easier-to-read sequence of Gm–E♭–D triads.

Because this sequence is resolving to D (despite being the V chord of the key of G that the song is in), let's analyze the sequence from the perspective that D is the I chord. (This is a common practice in classical and jazz analysis where multiple key signatures are thought of at once, and this will relate to something we've learned earlier, so please stick with me.) So, the analysis of the Gm–E♭–D triads is ivm–♭II–I. Where have we seen the ivm chord before? In the bridge section of "Perfectly Lonely" (pg. 66), where the Fm chord resolved to the C; this same concept is now propelling, and dramatizing, the resolution from the Gm (ivm) to the D chord (I chord) with an intermediary chord movement via a half step (i.e., E♭). Remember that we're moving towards the D chord (the V chord that holds a strong pull on the song we're in) and the ivm–♭II sequence made that resolution all the more powerful. The following diagram should give you a better idea of the thinking behind treating the V chord (D7) as a separate entity when composing your progressions.

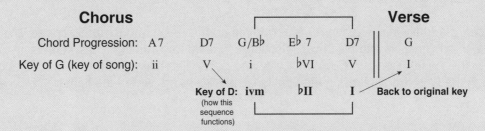

While this is a songwriting stretch, using formulas like this to dress up your progressions will add jazz and classical sophistication to your music, and John's demonstrated their value time and time again.

Verse 2

Despite having identical vocal content as its first iteration, the guitar work of verse 2 has noteworthy ideas in the final three measures. After a series of sparsely placed, chord-based double stops through measures 27–31, Gtr. 1 offers high-register fills and voice leading to usher in the restatement of the chorus. Over the G chord in measure 32, he repeatedly slides airy 6th shapes from the fifth and seventh frets on the G and E strings.

After a quick position shift in the latter half of measure 32, he hammers the fifth-position C/E chord and continues with an interesting harmonic choice: while holding the shape, he plays a descending line on the B string with each strum. Use a pinky–pinky–index fingering scheme for the 8–7–5 fret sequence (G–F♯–E) while accenting each top note so the line sounds more pronounced.

Guitar Solo

While Gtr. 1 lays down atmospheric chord rakes, Gtr. 2 makes its reappearance with a melodically understated solo. Restricting himself to the B string for the majority of the eight-measure G–C progression, Mayer fluidly navigates the G major pentatonic scale with Hendrix-inspired legato. Not only are they elegant major blues licks, but each one of them dovetails into the next, germinating into a larger idea.

Catching our ear right away, Mayer adopts a repeated motif (A–B, frets 10–12) with wide interval slides that vary in their higher extremities. Over the G chord, he expertly targets the 5th (D note, 15th fret) in measure 35 before returning to the 3rd (B note, 12th fret). Use an index–ring–slide for the 10–12–15 frets and then silently shift back to the 10th position with your ring finger for the hammer-pull maneuver that closes the phrase.

In preparation for the C chord in measure 37, he hints at the 3rd (E note, 17th fret) before taking his sweet time to eventually land on the 5th (G note, eighth fret) in measure 38. Use your ring finger for the slide from the 12th to eighth frets. For specifics on the technical foundation of legato string-slides, check out the "Pentatonic Articulations" subsection of the Integral Techniques chapter (page 113).

Not one to remain on an improvising idea for long, at measure 39, he establishes a D–E (fret 15–17) pedal tone idea on the B string. This motivic continuity is interspersed with accented A and B notes (frets 17 and 19) on the high E string. Once again, he varies the speed and spacing of the repetitions, gradually compacting them for a well-developed phrase. To physically pull off the wide stretches, use your index and ring fingers for the lower and higher frets of the B string, while your pinky pulls double-duty on the high E string.

Following the fifth D–E repetition, he closes the solo with a descending series of bends and slides. At measure 42, he plays 19th-fret, half-step bends that essentially serve as in-rhythm vibrato. Bending with the pinky is often tricky to keep in tune, so be wary of the tendency to over- or under-bend. After you play the 15th fret, E string with your index finger, quickly target the same fret on the B string with your ring finger in prep for the whole-step bends. More tricky, yet melodic, position shifts on the B string close out the solo, so be sure to check out the fill box on the bottom of page 77 for the location of the final C note.

Verse 3

Along with Mayer's more melismatic vocal liberties, verse 3 signals the beginning of the song's end with more aggressive fills from Gtr. 1. Faster rhythms and drastically pronounced articulations with wider interval choices gradually compound the arrangement texture towards the satisfying outro. Instead of waiting for the vocal spaces, Gtr. 1 constantly draws from the fill vocabulary of the previous verses, including low-string Gsus4 (i.e., G–B–C–D) arpeggio spellings and accented chord stabs (measures 44–45), staccato single notes with double stops based in C major pentatonic (measure 47), and shimmering 6th interval shapes (measure 48).

Notice how each idea gradually increases in *register* (moves up the neck) and rhythmic speed. Mayer clearly uses his fill opportunities, in conjunction with his vocal inflections, to build towards the lyrics, "Gravity has taken better men than me." After this recognition of his own mortality, the guitar fills revert to a more passive accompaniment by arpeggiating through the C/E chord, allowing the final lyrics of, "Keep me where the light is," to be easily heard.

Outro

Building on the growth that verse 3 started, the outro arrangement brings the dynamics to its ultimate fruition. As John vocally repeats the phrase, "Keep me where the light is," with ever-increasing blues melodies, not only do sustained chords and palm-muted double stops emerge (Gtrs. 3 and 4, respectively), but an appropriately selected gospel choir creates a heavenly ambience of "Oos" as Gtr. 1 adds tricky, double-stop fills.

In measures 52 and 53, Gtr. 1 starts a repeating, position-shifting riff of a G/B double stop and C/E arpeggio spelling. After you slide to the seventh fret, A string, barre the fifth fret with your index finger and then jump back to third position, grabbing the G and B strings with your middle and index fingers, respectively.

At measure 55, John moves an interesting combination of triple and double stops down the G Dorian mode. Played over the C change, this line implies a C9 harmony, being the first time we hear this technical and harmonic deviation. He resolves the line on beat 1 of measure 56 after a surprise bluesy triplet.

For measures 57–58, Gtr. 1 revisits the position-shifting idea from measure 52 and expounds on it with hammered double stops. The double stops incorporate stretches and tricky right-hand techniques, so isolate both finger-twisting moves before you tackle measure 57 in its entirety. The double stops hammer into a B/D dyad from the A note—a move we learned for the intro (page 71). Allowing the B-string note to ring as you hammer requires careful arching, so experiment with your hand position, leaning your knuckles a little more toward the ceiling if things sound muted. Once the double stops are sounding smooth, the C7 arpeggio with a ♭9th ornament should be a breeze, but play the eighth fret, D string with your pinky to stay in position. Gtr. 1 draws back for the fade out at measure 59, but Mayer continues to wail the most enduring lyrical message to close his biggest hit.

Gravity
Full Song

GRAVITY

Words and Music by John Mayer

*Chord symbols reflect basic harmony.
**T = Thumb on 6th string.

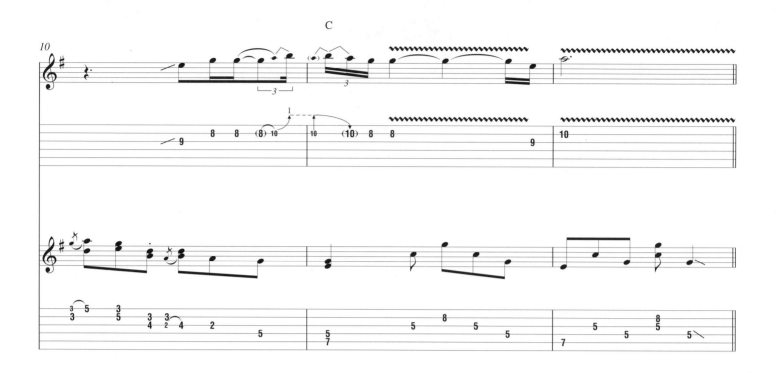

Verse
Gtr. 2 tacet

1. Grav - i - ty___ is work - ing a - gainst me,___

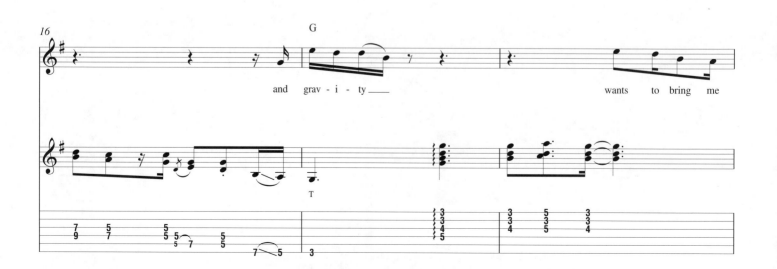

and grav - i - ty___ wants to bring me

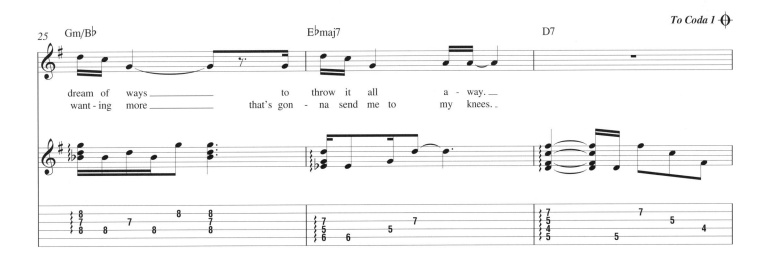

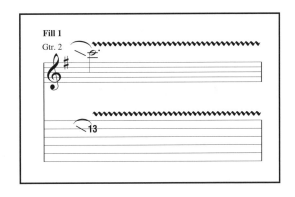

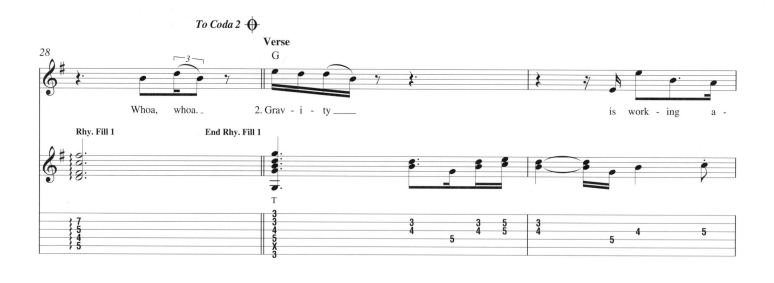

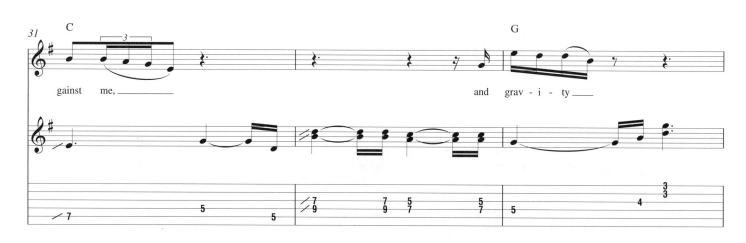

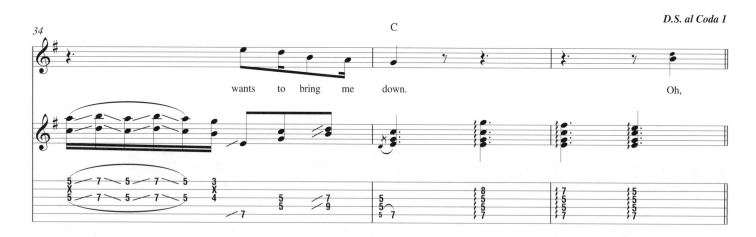

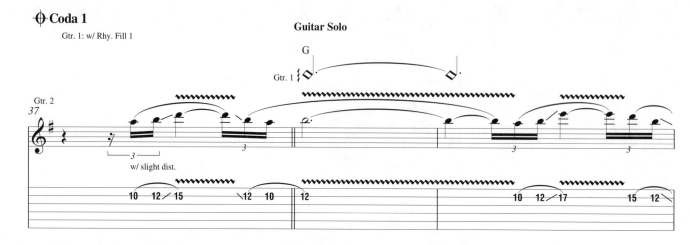

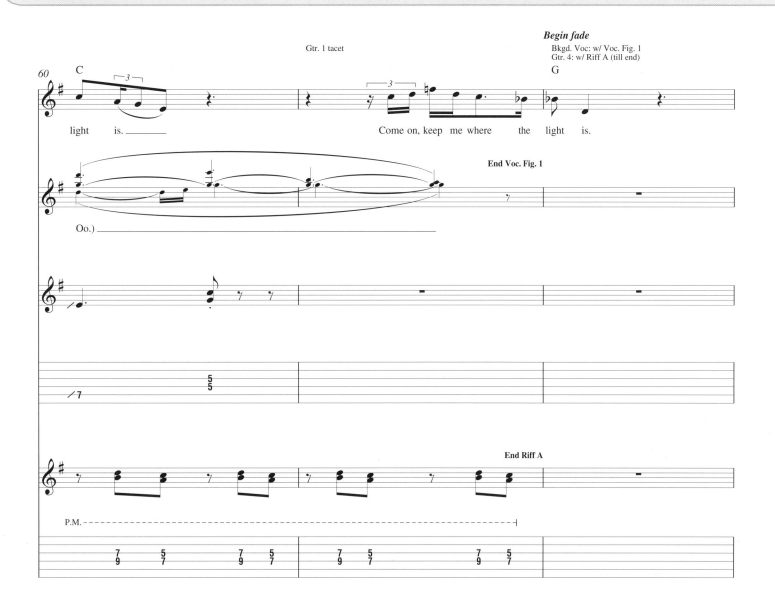

light is. _____ Come on, keep me where the light is.

Oo.) _____

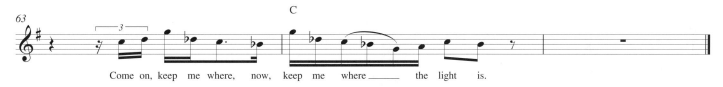

Come on, keep me where, now, keep me where _____ the light is.

ESSENTIAL LICKS

Here, we'll uncover the musical nuggets that consistently show up in John's improvisations. While the licks are primarily influence-based, his assimilation of those influences, filtered through his melodic sensibilities within a modern pop context, provides the individuality of his lines. Because of this clear distinction of soloing material, this chapter is divided into two sections: Influence Interpretation and Pentatonic Melodicism. In the former, we'll look at those who shaped his guitar personality and how his personality re-shaped their licks. Then, the latter will expose how he abandons the box shape for melodically rich ideas. Essentially, these sections divide the licks into positional playing and those times he navigates the entirety of the neck, but the focus of the analysis is on how he adopted those concepts into his own artistry.

Influence Interpretation

Not one of us learned guitar in a vacuum. We endlessly pored over albums, lesson materials, and tablature books in the unending quest to sound like those who inspired us to play. Things were no different for John Mayer's formative years when he was copying B.B. King's "butterfly" vibrato and octave slides, Jimi Hendrix's rhythm parts, and Stevie Ray Vaughan's powerful pentatonics. But after living and breathing their licks for years, he took things a step further to eventually morph the intent of those licks to suit his unique expression on the instrument.

In this section, we'll examine the licks of his iconic blues influences and how he shaped them into something all his own. While the analysis weighs heavily on the influence of the legends, the licks themselves are inspired by John's live solos with his phrasing. So when two licks are not contrasted side by side, you can be sure it's a genuine "Mayerism."

Stevie Ray Vaughan

No one coaxed more power and signature licks out of the pentatonic scale than Stevie Ray Vaughan. This Texas titan of the Stratocaster single-handedly revitalized the blues in the mid-'80s with his fierce tone and aggressive style. His manipulation of this five-note scale perked up the ears and inspired countless "Vaughan-abees," with Mayer being one of the most authentic.

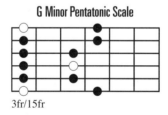

Lick 1

One of SRV's more impressive displays of scale mastery is how he seamlessly drops (or raises) the box shape an octave in the middle of a phrase. Here, the G minor pentatonic is first bluesified at the 15th position in a typical manner. Then, without missing a beat, he finishes the lick at the third position with an instantaneous, 12-fret index-finger slide down into the lower octave.

Lick 2

Continuing with the idea of position-shifting, SRV would often follow sustained notes with blink-of-an-eye pull-offs. These quick, "pentatonic falls" are effective for closing phrases or giving unexpected motion to a flowing line. Here, they accent the G–D–Bb notes of a Gm chord with descending legato from the sixth to third positions of the same pentatonic scale.

*Hammer on from nowhere

Lick 3

He would also incorporate a b9th trill into his minor pentatonic fare. In beat 2 the G–Ab–G hammer-pull on the E string functions as an accented ornament before the piercing, Albert King bends. This is a pretty hip extension over the dominant chord and accentuates the bluesy feel of this lick, even more so than the b5th.

Lick 4

While John would quote the b9th ornament in his slow blues, he would use the ♮9th in uptempo shuffles where the harmony was more major than dominant.

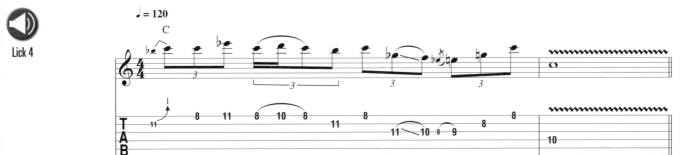

While the previous licks were centered on the first position of the minor pentatonic, Stevie, and John, would cop their best Albert King impression out of the upper extension of the minor pentatonic box. The ninth fret, E string of this shape (C# note; highlighted) has been the primary target of their bending endeavors to great emotional effect.

A Minor Pentatonic Scale
(upper extension w/optional note)

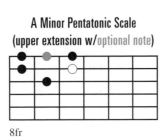

8fr

Lick 5

Measure 1 features varying bending degrees on frets 8–10 of the E string, played with one finger per fret. Measure 2 is where the fun begins with double-stop bends. To add the extra girth with minimal effort, you have to catch the B string under the tip of your ring finger as you bend the E string to its final pitch. It's almost like using bad technique; you would normally mute the neighboring string as you push up. But for this, once you see the E string touch the B, angle your hand back, lifting the fingertip, without releasing pressure from the fretboard. Here's how the strings look when properly merged together:

You only need to do this once, at the beginning of measure 2, because when you move to different frets, you only need to maintain the closeness of the strings under your fingers.

Lick 5

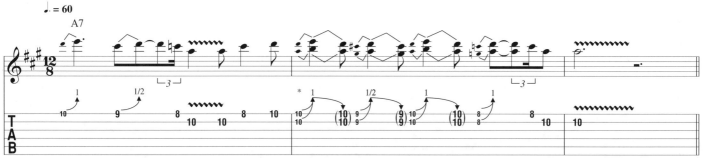

*Allow B string to be caught under ring, middle & index fingers for bends.

Jimi Hendrix

Lick 6

Taking the pentatonic scale into the realms of rhythm, Jimi Hendrix infused his accompaniment methods with R&B-style fills, sliding 4ths, and hammered double stops to great effect in his power trio ensemble (bass, drums, and guitar). The following is a rhythmic study of the inflections he'd use. As you can hear, beats 1 and 2 are primarily chord stabs that establish the harmony, while the remainder of the measure showcases the variety of fills available from that shape.

Despite the changing Dm–Gm–Dm progression, the fills are derived from the same pentatonic shape. After you've learned the licks for each chord, try transposing them to the other (i.e., move the sliding 4ths idea in measure 3 to the 10th-position Dm chord, etc.).

Throughout example, fret all notes on 6th string w/ thumb.

B.B. King

B.B. King was the master of the unison/octave. His phrases often ended with playing a note and then playing that same note on a different string with his stingingly fast vibrato. Mayer employs a similar device with a variation in articulation. As heard in his solo from "Perfectly Lonely," Mayer arrives at the same note through a bend, then a slide. This subtle yet unique adaptation of an iconic lick shows how a simple change in articulation can pay homage to an influence without direct plagiarism.

Lick 7

This classic B.B. idea starts at the third position G minor pentatonic with a ring-finger bend on the G string that crosses through a 5th–root ascent before quickly sliding to the root at the eighth fret of the B string. Before reverting back to the original position with a quick, legato descent, he adds his signature "hummingbird" vibrato for the most magical of sustain.

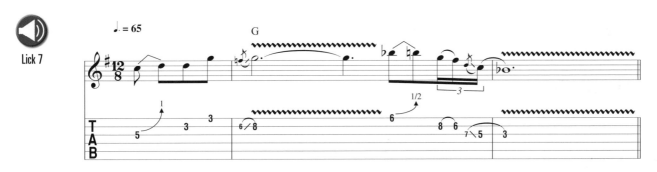

Lick 8

With Mayer's interpretation of the lick, he would often replace B.B.'s trademark vibrato with a bend directly followed by a slide, providing a sustain quality all its own. What's happening here is that he bends, releases it, then instantly slides up to the note to which he bent. For this series of moves to remain effective as two notes, the release needs to happen as you slide up. To perform this, don't worry about releasing the bend because as you're sliding up (i.e., moving your ring finger from the sixth to the eighth fret), you naturally release the bend.

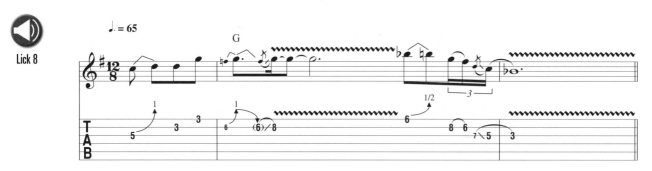

B.B. Box

Because of its iconic use on the frets of his prized axe, "Lucille," B.B.'s application of this elegant major/minor mixing scale form has become his undeniable stamp on all players questing to find the melodic sweetness of the blues. Below is the B.B. box in C at the 12th position. Here, the major sounds of the 9th (D: 15th fret, string 2) and 6th (A: 14th fret, string 3) are comfortably nested by the tart ♭3rd (E♭: 16th fret, string 2) of the blues, to which is commonly applied a half-step bend to suggest the major 3rd (E: 12th fret, string 1).

B.B. Box (Key of C)

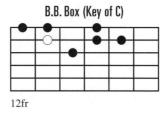

12fr

Lick 9

Here's a lick based out of the B.B. Box that capitalizes on the interplay of the A/E♭ tritone on strings 3 and 2. Starting with a whole-step bend to E, the lick features a pedal-point idea that alternates the A note on the 14th fret, G string with a descending line on the B string from E♭ to C. For the wide, 12th- to 16th-fret stretch at the end of beat 1, use your index and pinky fingers, respectively.

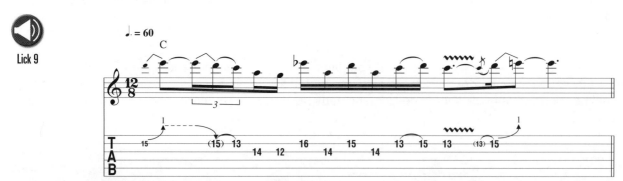

Pentatonic Melodicism

The remainder of the licks will primarily focus on Mayer's melodic sense derived from the pentatonic scale. Repeating licks, double stops, and more flood his solos for dramatic consistency and rhythmic variety.

Lick 10

Often heard in his 16th-shuffle grooves, John adds one-measure riffs like this over his changing chord progressions. Similar to "Your Body Is a Wonderland," this fragment is designed as a complementary part to an eighth-note-based rhythm part (using open-position chords), filling the arrangement "holes." Based in the D major pentatonic scale in seventh position, this lick features sliding 4th intervals on the "and" of beat 3. Barre the dyad at fret 7 with your index finger and move your whole hand in rhythm as you slide back and forth.

Lick 10

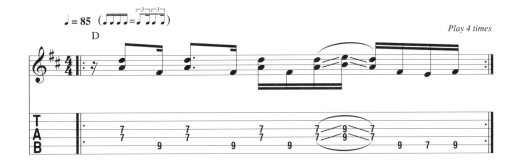

Lick 11

Enhancing the lyrical quality of his lines, Mayer uses slides to not only move around the neck, but also to re-articulate the same note. Similar to the B.B.-inspired bend-slide maneuver, grace-note slides allow for extra sustain when the notes are held for a considerable length of time. This sustain is particularly effective for double stops.

Akin to his Hendrix-inspired fills from "Gravity" and "Bold as Love," this lick is based out of the extension of the eighth-position G major pentatonic scale, sliding into the B/D dyad and accenting beat 2 with an additional slide.

Lick 11

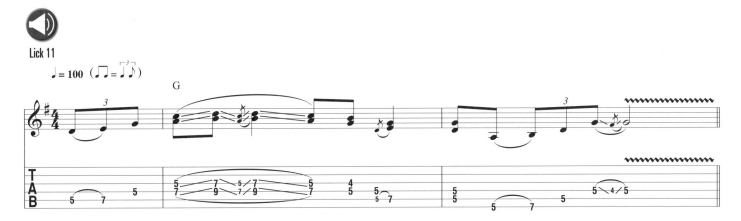

Lick 12

This one doesn't find its way into John's style as a lick, per se, but more as a textural through line in a harmonically active chord progression. Similar to the bridge of "Slow Dancing in a Burning Room" (played by Gtr. 9), serial bends and releases like this usually move from the 3rd to the 4th of a chord—in this case, a G#–A bend over an E. Beat 4 augments the half-step bends with a wider minor 3rd (1-1/2 steps), followed by a smooth slide down to the fifth fret. Check against the fretted equivalents for proper bending intonation, remembering that a half step equals one fret.

Lick 12

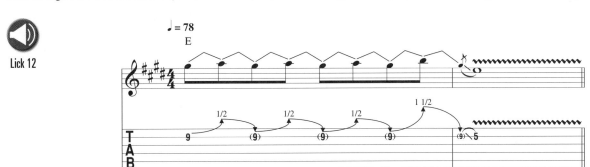

Lick 13

Serial bends can be memorable opening statements, as well—especially with this melodically expressive version, à la Jeff Beck. Not only do the bends smoothly release, but they also raise, add vibrato, and then raise some more in vocal-like fashion. Based in the extension box at the 11th-position C minor pentatonic scale, this lick is mainly heard in John's slow blues or pop contexts. In measure 1, bend the whole step with your ring, sustain it with a little wiggle, and then, without releasing, bend another half step before you finally release the whole way in rhythm. The bend and overbend moves work best if you have the sound in your ears and feeling in your hands, so practice the whole step and minor 3rd bends by themselves before you work on the bending series.

Next, trill from the 11th to the 13th frets with your index and ring, follow it down the E♭ arpeggio, and climb back up to the 10th fret with an index-finger roll on strings 4 and 3. The final measure sees another rhythmic overbend sandwiched between a vibratoed, grace-note hammer-on to an instant pull-off. Make sure that the pull-off is quick enough so the note on the 12th fret is imperceptible.

Lick 14

Double-stop ornaments like this become more impressive when played in triplet- and 16th-note rhythms. This lick deftly maneuvers through G major pentatonic with tricky fingerings for the constant double stops that cap the lick. To get your left hand in shape, isolate the hammer-ons with the fingerings (provided underneath the tab staff), as the position-shifting and stretches make this one a finger-twister.

Lick 15

Unison bends are often used in John's solos as separately picked rhythmic ideas. Keeping the notes from ringing into each other is the secret behind the rhythm, so use the pick-hand palm to control the sustain of the bend and release pressure from your index finger to keep the 10th fret, E string quiet.

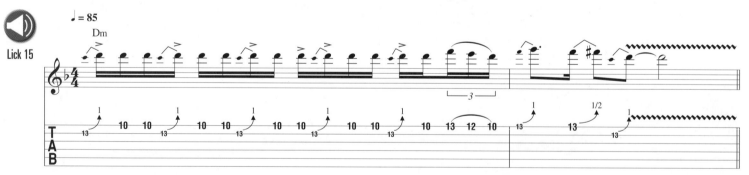

Lick 16

To build up tension to a solo's ending, Mayer often uses repeating fragments like this over changing chords. Played over a D chord, the lick opens with a 3rd–root–5th idea that moves towards a bluesy climax with bends and a tricky descending minor pentatonic sequence. He'd get a lot of harmonic mileage out of a simple germ of an idea by commonly starting the fragment on the IV chord (G chord) and continuing it through the I (D).

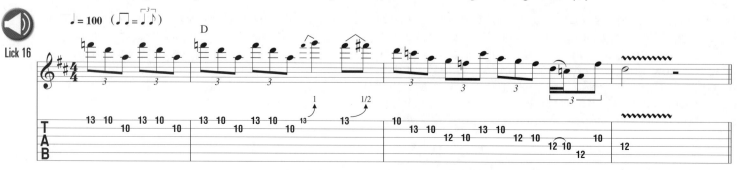

Lick 17

Most of the ideas so far have been relatively localized to one position for the entirety of the lick. But what mystifies new players, more often than not, is how soloists seamlessly traverse the extremes of the neck's geography. Based on the position-shifting heard and seen in many of his live solos, it's likely that John is aware of *symmetrical fingerings*. This method of quickly seeing the fretboard as a network of intertwining patterns is easy to remember because, when you switch strings at the appropriate places, the fingerings repeat as you move up the neck. Here, we have a G major arpeggio that spans three octaves, and each one is indicated with different dots on the diagram. Play the shape with an index–pinky–middle fretting scheme for each octave and repeat the fingering as you ascend.

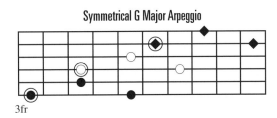

Symmetrical G Major Arpeggio

Here, we apply the fingering to a dramatic ascent in triplets, climaxing at the 15th position with a G major/minor mixing lick. The position shifts quickly target the arpeggio notes via whole-step slides played with the ring finger, but the shift on beat 3 requires distinct scripting. While frets 10 and 12 lend themselves to index and ring finger placement, the slide from fret 12 to fret 15 is performed with the index finger to allow for the comfortable continuation of the pentatonic blues bends at the 18th fret with the ring finger.

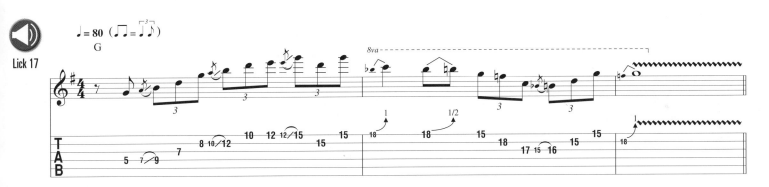

Lick 18

Another position-shifting workout, this lick descends in major pentatonic-derived double stops before bluesing things up at the third position, addressing the ♭3rd, ♭5th, and ♭7th with two-finger legato. With the solo and fills from "Gravity" under your hands, the G major and minor pentatonics shouldn't be anything new, but beat 3 of measure 1 once again boasts unconventional fingering. After you use your index–ring for the 5–7 hammer-on, grab fret 5 on the D string with your middle, freeing up your index to reach back to fret 3 of the G string, deftly moving you back to the third position to finish the blues scale descent.

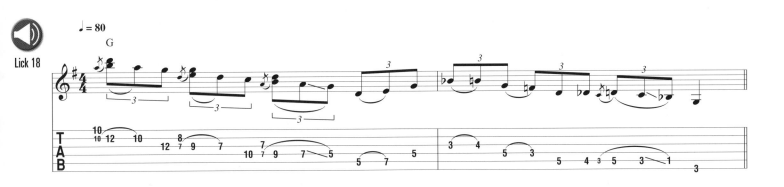

Lick 19

With his loose right hand and flawless fret-hand muting, John's use of rakes in his lead lines adds forward motion and interest to his descending lines. This G major pentatonic lick moves from the eighth to fifth position with reverse rakes, slides, and hammer-ons. The rakes themselves move through different inversions of C and G chords, so familiarize yourself with the chord shapes before practicing the raking motion.

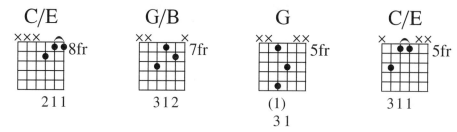

Rakes are similar to sweeping, where the pick grazes the strings in one fluid motion, as opposed to picking, where you articulate each note. So, plucking each individual string would rob the lick of its needed flow.

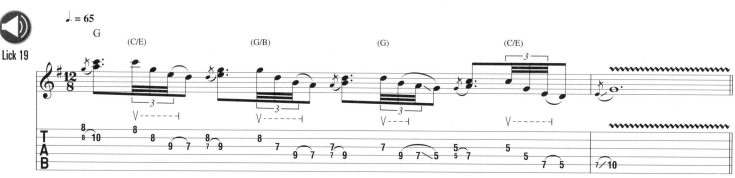

Lick 20

When Mayer plays more melodically, he typically restricts himself to single-string lines where his legato takes center stage. Heard in his solos from the studio releases of "Gravity" and "Waiting on the World to Change," his favorite device is a whole-step hammer-on to a wide-interval slide. This lick is a sequential descent of the G major pentatonic on the B string with ring-finger slides that vary from 4th to 5th intervals (15th to 10th fret and eighth to third fret, respectively). To increase your sliding accuracy, train your eye to focus on where your sliding finger is going—not where it is. For instance, on the hammer-slide of beat 2, keep your eye on the 10th fret and not the hammer-on. Use your ears for the hammer-on and your eyes for the slide's target fret. Always thinking one or two notes ahead of where you are will enhance your expression on the instrument.

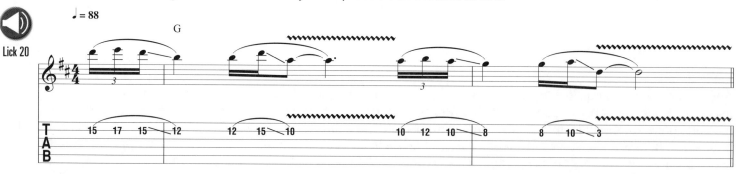

Lick 21

String skipping ideas help break up his pentatonic scale playing into unexpected sequences. Drawing from the A minor pentatonic scale with a momentary allusion to the blues (E♭: fret 8, string 3), this lick is made up of three six-note descents from the G, E, and C notes. The pull-offs create a tricky picking pattern where you use an upstroke prior to the string skip.

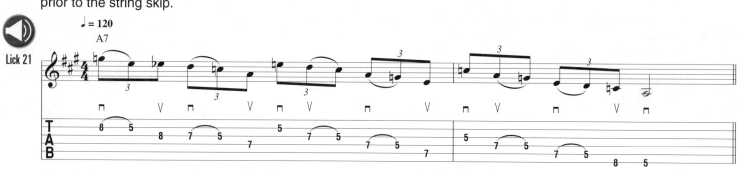

Lick 22

Being an excellent lead player while interjecting chord stabs into his solos and vice versa, John's constant awareness of the underlying harmony is apparent through his mix of pentatonics and arpeggios within a single phrase. The next couple of licks will hinge on this E-shape arpeggio at the eighth fret (C chord).

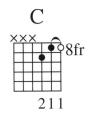

Played in an uptempo blues shuffle, this bluesy C minor pentatonic lick opens by approaching the shape via a half step to land the E note on the beat. Where the remainder of the lick is more minor in tonality, the spelling of the arpeggio shape is enough to imply the major harmony and the soloing sophistication that goes with it.

Lick 23

Sliding into that shape and then descending the minor pentatonic can also be used as an effective ending for the last few measures of a 12-bar blues. This lick transposes the same Mixolydian idea to the G7 and F7 chords (V and IV chords) as a continuity device over disparate harmonies and effectively prepares for the triplet rhythms of the C chord (I).

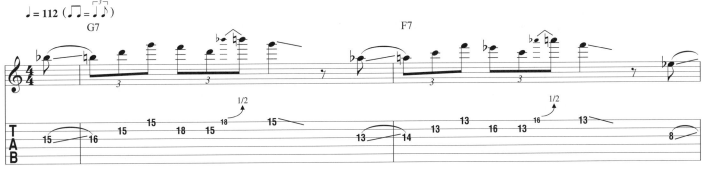

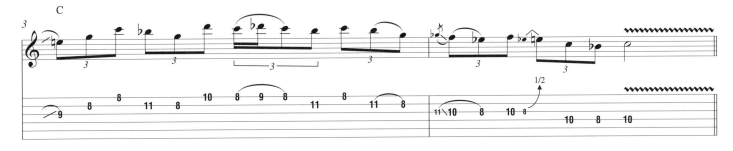

ESSENTIAL RIFFS

From Mayer's debut *Room for Squares* to his musically confident *Continuum*, the breadth of technical and melodic variety present in his songs offers a masterclass in arrangement construction, riff structure, and rhythmic interest. These ten classics chronologically display his guitar maturity by running the gamut from simple acoustic fingerpicking and effect-reliant riffing to aggressive, power trio blues.

Why Georgia
From *Room for Squares*, 2001

Following his brief, two-semester music education at Berklee, John worked the Atlanta club scene for two years before he was eventually discovered in 2000. When money was short and opportunities were few, John's inspiration for "Why Georgia" was born out of the uncertainty he experienced. Fortunately, the song eventually became his third single, and the acoustic intro is one of his best.

Mayer opens the song with a G–D riff where cool tricks like hammer-ons and open strings create sus2 and add4 qualities. While the Gsus2 chord's parent shape is easily identifiable, the Dadd4 is based on a common C shape moved up two frets. Using your ring finger for the A string and the middle finger for the D string will not only help retain fingering form, but aid in smooth position shifting as well.

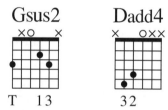

With these shapes in hand, the right-hand role of this riff brings a depth of coolness to a self-contained performance on acoustic. While your fingers typically take care of the higher-string notes on the offbeats (individually or simultaneously), your thumb is the key to getting the groove across.

On beat 1, the thumb plucks the low E string (simple enough) and then your fingers take care of the hammered double stop. But beats 2 and 4 introduce a new technique called *thumb slapping*. Simulating a typical snare drum pattern, you bring your thumb down onto the strings hard enough that they add a percussive effect to the groove by slapping against the frets. For more details on how this is performed, see the Accompaniment section of the Integral Techniques chapter to get your hand in shape, as you'll also need it to get the feel down for "Neon."

In order to make the transition smooth from the Gsus2 to the Dadd4 chord, take advantage of the open A string for switching. Then pluck the dyad on beat 3 with your thumb and middle finger. This will open your fingers up for plucking the open-G string with the ring and then arpeggiating the successive strings of beat 4 with a thumb slap–index–middle–ring pattern.

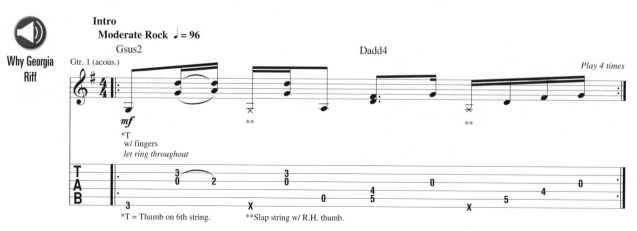

Neon
From *Room for Squares*, 2001

John's musical efforts in Atlanta were spent as a songwriting duo with fellow Berklee alum and brief songwriting partner, Clay Cook. With this bare-bones ensemble, John's rhythmic sense came to light with the grooving funk of "Neon." Played on his SRV strat for the studio cut from *Room for Squares*, John ditches his pick for a challenging riff of unconventional technique.

The intro riff uses a drop C tuning, where the E string is lowered by two whole steps to C (a minor 3rd). Unlike most dropped tunings that have an open-string equivalent (e.g., drop D, drop B, etc.), this tuning uses the third fret, A string as a pitch reference for the 12th-fret harmonic of the E string. If you have a guitar with a floating bridge (i.e., a whammy bar), check the remaining strings after you lower the string to C, as the tension of the neck will have changed, causing those strings to go flat.

The intro is a funky, two-measure riff based on five chords. Csus4 and E♭sus2 are pretty simple grips:

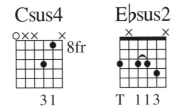

The remaining chords provide the biggest potential for pain. The thumb fretting Mayer uses is unique, as most chords have the thumb fret the lowest-numbered fret of the shape (e.g., first position, F chord), but the Fm11 and B♭6/9 chords require thumb fretting on the higher-numbered frets of the shape. While this is a comfortably natural position for John's huge hands, for us less-endowed, these grips may be a physical impossibility and a performance hindrance. So below each shape, I've included an alternate fingering that replaces the thumb with the ring finger and incorporates the pinky. Before tackling the tab, focus on memorizing the chord forms and switching them smoothly through the positions. Then you'll feel if the alternate fingerings work for you.

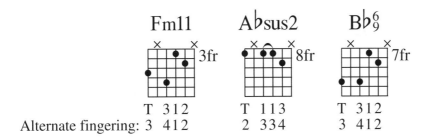

While the left hand has potentially painful physical hurdles, the role of the right hand brings another level of complexity. Live videos show him alternating between thumb slapping and index-finger plucking despite the string crossing. This requires slow practice, proper hand position, and consistent accuracy while gradually building the tempo up, so head on over to the Accompaniment section of the Integral Techniques chapter for drills and suggestions to help you sink further into the groove.

Neon Riff

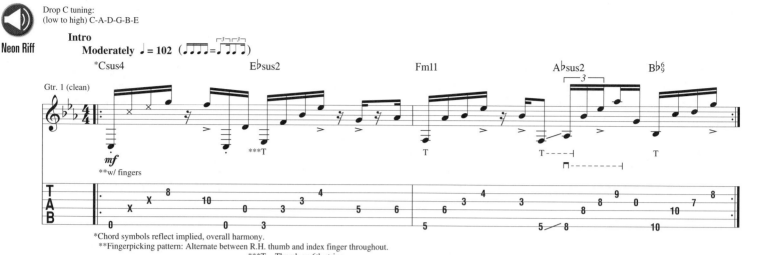

Drop C tuning:
(low to high) C-A-D-G-B-E

Intro
Moderately ♩ = 102

*Chord symbols reflect implied, overall harmony.
**Fingerpicking pattern: Alternate between R.H. thumb and index finger throughout.
***T = Thumb on 6th string.

Words and Music by John Mayer and Clay Cook
Copyright © 1999 Specific Harm Music and Me Hold You Music
All Rights on behalf of Specific Harm Music Administered by Goodium Music, Inc., c/o Cal Financial Group, 700 Harris Street, Suite 201, Charlottesville, VA 22903
International Copyright Secured   All Rights Reserved

Your Body Is a Wonderland
From *Room for Squares*, 2001

Clearly an ode to the fairer sex and responsible for attracting legions of female fans, "Your Body Is a Wonderland" went on to win a Grammy for John's debut album, *Room for Squares*. The song's intro features a well-constructed riff and is an excellent example of how to effectively arrange guitar parts.

Both guitars are in drop D tuning, in which the low-E string is "dropped" by a whole step to D. If you're only choosing to play along with Gtr. 2 for now, don't worry about lowering the E string, as the lick only has you fretting the D through B strings. When you're ready to tackle the rhythm part and you don't have a tuner, simply tune the 12th-fret harmonic of the low-E string to your open D string; they'll be in the same octave and vibrate in unison when tuned.

Gtr. 1 (acous.) provides the framework for the intro with a two-measure riff that alternates between bass and chordal punches and is fingerpicked in a quirky, eighth-note rhythm. Based on F5, Csus4, and B♭sus2 chord forms, it features a walking bassline and common tones (shown as white circles), making simple fingerings by virtue of the tuning. Mayer typically plays this part with a thumb slap on beats 2 and 4.

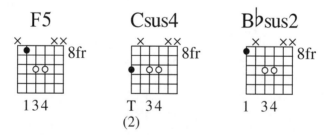

While the acoustic provides a solid foundation, the clean electric fills the holes with an upper-register, "popcorn" lick (palm-muted 16th notes) with sliding dyads from the 10th-position F major pentatonic scale. Here are the notes relevant to the line, and the common tones from the chord shapes are, once again, shown as white circles:

F Major Scale (w/ common tones)

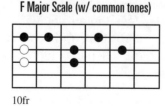

10fr

Playing through each of these parts is fun, but when you hear them mixed together, the contrast between each and how they fit together is largely due to how the parts are constructed. The acoustic's low-register, two-measure figure has a warmer, dutiful sound, while the electric's high-register, one-measure lick provides a rubbing constancy over the B♭sus2 and Csus4 chords of measure 2. Building your arrangements with similar and unique material—e.g., higher and lower, sustained and muted, busy and laid-back—allows you to fill more sonic space, and Mayer did just that for this catchy pop tune.

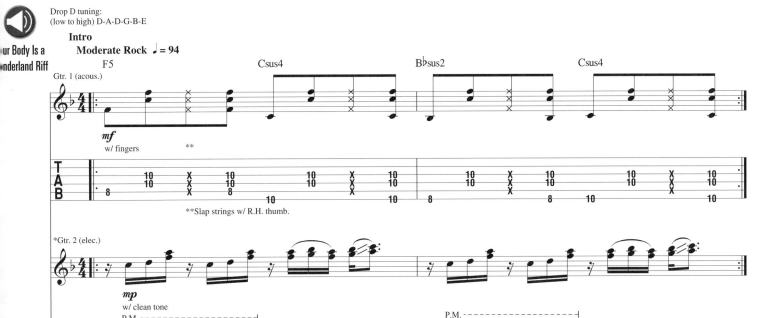

Drop D tuning:
(low to high) D-A-D-G-B-E

ur Body Is a
nderland Riff

My Stupid Mouth
From *Room for Squares*, 2001

The intro to "My Stupid Mouth" features an unaccompanied acoustic as an example of understated rhythm playing at its finest. It has contrapuntal basslines, common chord tones, and is a beautiful study in complex harmonies within a simplistic context.

The diatonic, four-measure D5–A/C♯, D–Gsus2, Bm7–F♯m7, Gsus2 progression is based on these familiar, open-position chords.

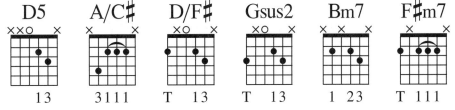

Once again, John's go-to groove of swung 16ths is at work to great effect. Most of the harmonic movement occurs on the offbeat (A/C♯, D/F♯, and F♯m7), and the tail-end of measure 2 features a subtle D–E fill while holding the surrounding Gsus2 shape.

As if that intrigue wasn't enough, these chords, inherent to their sequence, have underlying qualities that bear thorough investigation. Most apparent is the bassline, shown by the chord names (root names in boldface: **D**5–**A**/C♯– **D**/F♯–**G**sus2, **B**m7–**F**♯m7–**G**sus2). Playing the notes individually will help you appreciate the intervallic jumps at work and give you a feel for the offbeat chord changes.

My Stupid Mouth
Example 1

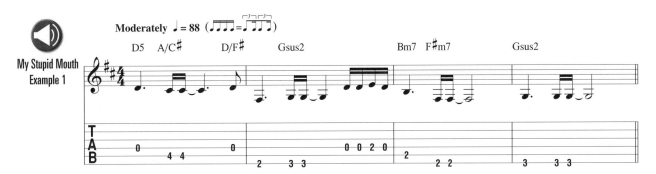

Atop the bassline is an additional element of continuity. If you look at each of the six individual chords, you'd notice that strings 4–2 have fingerings that move between only two shapes. They alternate between D/A/D (common to D5, D/F♯, Gsus2, and Bm7), D/A/C♯ (common to A/C♯ and F♯m7), and back to D/A/D in a two-measure pattern. The open D string runs as a common thread throughout, but it doesn't really affect the intended harmony of the A/C♯ and F♯m7 chords.

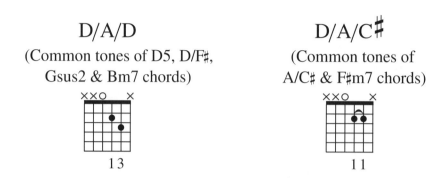

Suffice it to say that the bassline, common tones, and the infectious groove of this progression have all the elements that make up a solid foundation of interesting rhythm playing.

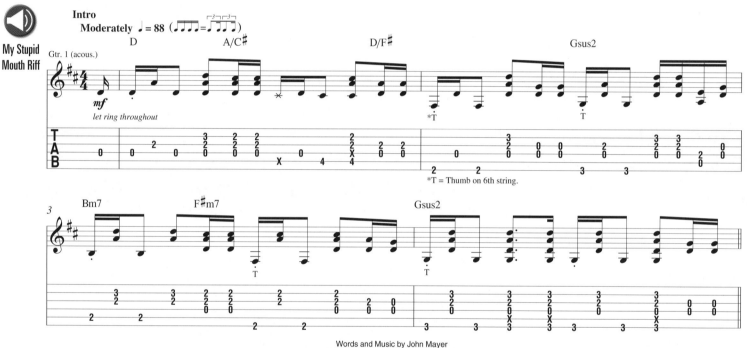

Words and Music by John Mayer
Copyright © 1999 Specific Harm Music
All Rights Administered by Goodium Music, Inc., c/o Cal Financial Group, 700 Harris Street, Suite 201, Charlottesville, VA 22903
International Copyright Secured   All Rights Reserved

Bigger Than My Body
From *Heavier Things*, 2003

After touring for two years straight in promotion of the acoustic-heavy *Room for Squares*, Mayer's electrically charged follow-up, *Heavier Things*, lives up to its name in both musical soundscape and lyrical content. "Bigger Than My Body" was the first single off the album, and its music video set the tone for the rest of the album with a satisfying message and a melodic intro hook.

Gtr. 1 is a simple, hybrid picking riff that follows the verse's eight-measure melody. It features a descending E Mixolydian line with a droning open E string in between. With measures 1–4 fretted exclusively on the G string, the notes on the seventh, sixth, and fourth frets can be played with the pinky, ring, and index fingers, respectively. In measure 2, shift your index finger to fret 1, setting up your middle finger to easily grab fret 2. However, at the second ending (measure 5), when you've played measure 2 for the second time, shift your index finger up to fret 2, and you'll be in position to play the descending line with your ring and index finger on frets 4 and 2 of the D string, respectively.

While the descending line shouldn't give you too much trouble, the open E string throws a hair in the rhythm. Because it's natural to think the pick strokes need to land on the beats, the inverted nature of the riff takes some getting used to.

John achieves the unique distorted tone using an AdrenaLinn I pedal. Gtr. 2 is an arrangement of the line that was programmed into the pedal's sequencer section. While the settings to generate the lick and its tone are complicated and exclusive to the pedal, the tone can be achieved with a tremolo (set to eighth notes) and phaser pedal when overdubbed by your good-ol' six-string. For the line itself, it's part of a two-measure loop, comfortably set in the second-position A major pentatonic scale and played in 16th-note legato with the index and ring fingers.

Bigger Than My Body Riff

*AdrenaLinn pedal arr. for gtr.
**Chord symbols reflect overall harmony.
***Tremolo set for eighth-note regeneration.

Words and Music by John Mayer
Copyright © 2003 Specific Harm Music
All Rights Administered by Goodium Music, Inc., c/o Cal Financial Group, 700 Harris Street, Suite 201, Charlottesville, VA 22903
International Copyright Secured   All Rights Reserved

Something's Missing
From *Heavier Things*, 2003

"Something's Missing" takes inventory of how new-found fame leaves gaps in personal fulfillment, and the rolling intro riff loops with that same circular feeling. Gtr. 1 is in an altered tuning (Esus2 tuning), which raises the A and D strings by a whole step (to B and E, respectively) and lowers the G string by a half step to F♯. If you don't have a tuner, follow this procedure:

1. Hold down the fourth fret, D string and tune the open G string to match it.
2. Match the 12th-fret harmonic on the A string to the open B string.
3. Finally, sound the 12th-fret harmonic of the low E string and tune the D string to the same note.
4. To check yourself once you're close, remember that your reference note for the third string (formerly G, now F♯) has changed tuning as well, so use the second fret, 4th string (formerly D, now E) once the others are solid to your ears.

The intro is an eight-measure vamp in C♯m composed of a repeating two-measure phrase that's played by a clean-tone Strat with the neck and middle pickups. The first measure consists of a sustained *reverse rake* of a C♯m11 chord. While the name sounds complicated, the tuning makes it easy work for the index finger. The reverse rake is kind of like a strum, but the pick grazes the strings in a slower fashion to the point that the individual notes of the chord are more distinct.

The second measure of the phrase involves a three-note riff of two open strings between a descending bass line played in 16th notes. Let the open strings ring as your index and ring fingers hold the second and fourth frets, respectively, and experiment with whether *alternate picking* (down-up picking) or *economy picking* (i.e., down–down–up) works better as you negotiate beats 1–3. Beat 4 rounds out the syncopated riff with a pair of pull-offs that nicely fit the beat.

At measure 5, Gtr. 2 enters with a soft, complementary part. In standard tuning, it joins in on the rakes of beat 2 with a lush C♯m9 voicing. The interplay between the fretted and open strings is what Mayer capitalizes on with this chord, so be sure that you arch your pinky enough to let the high E string ring.

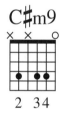

In measure 6, Gtr. 2 continues with a syncopated D♯–E droning texture that adds even more rhythmic complexity to the two-against-three feel of Gtr. 1's bass-string activity. Continue to hold the shape down as you pick the open and fretted strings to maintain the vibrancy of this understated riff.

Something's Missing
Riff

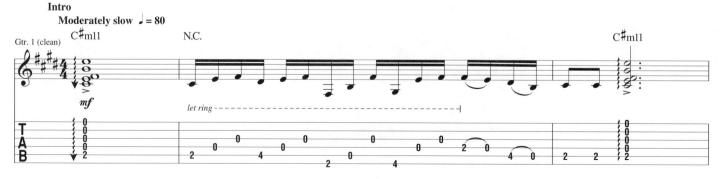

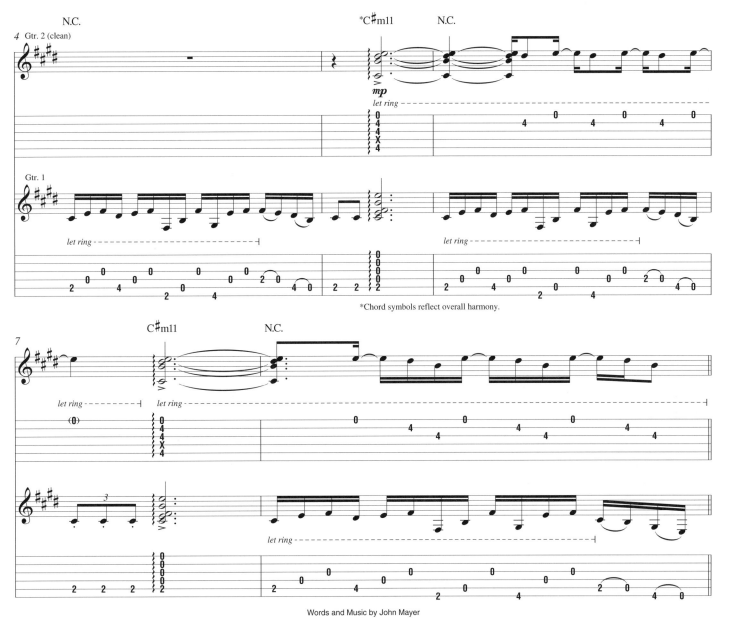

*Chord symbols reflect overall harmony.

Words and Music by John Mayer
Copyright © 2003 Specific Harm Music
All Rights Administered by Goodium Music, Inc., c/o Cal Financial Group, 700 Harris Street, Suite 201, Charlottesville, VA 22903
International Copyright Secured   All Rights Reserved

Try
From *Try!*, 2005

The first of two original tunes from the John Mayer Trio, "Try" brings the explosive drumming of Steve Jordan, the thumping bass of Pino Palladino, and the aggressive riffing of John Mayer to the forefront of uptempo blues. Lyrically telling the thought process of trying to impress a girl by being himself, "Try" is a metaphor for Mayer's refocused musical priorities by staying true to his blues roots. How well this trio plays off each other is amazing, and the fact that they're playing live reaffirms their formidable talents.

The intro is a stand-out display of John's finely honed power trio blues playing, where he's essentially playing rhythm and lead at the same time. For the first 30 seconds, Mayer plays an unaccompanied C-chord vamp with two beats each of bluesy chord stabs and dizzying pentatonics. After Steve hammers an aggressive two-measure drum fill, Pino's bass and John's custom ES-335 add harmonic structure to establish the song's repeating C–Am–F7 vamp, which is based on these chord forms.

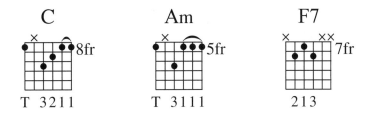

Much like his initial strategy, Mayer incorporates the chords into his muted riffing on beats 3 and 4 from an eighth-position mix of C major and minor pentatonics. He doesn't use the entirety of both scales with the brief chances that he gets for fills, but here's a scale-combining layout that shows both scales side by side and how he translates them into split-second fills.

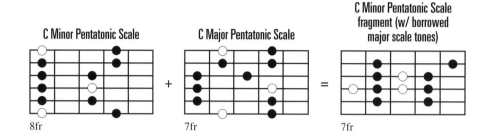

Gtr. 2, played by Chalmers Alford, adds sparse, higher-register fills based primarily at the 12th position. Finding the holes in the latter half of each measure, he adds hammered double stops, sliding 6ths, and technically challenging single-note lines to blur the musical sense of who's playing what. Notable instances of these fortuitous sonic illusions are in measures 2, 6, and 8, where Chalmers' double stops add upper extensions to Mayer's rhythm.

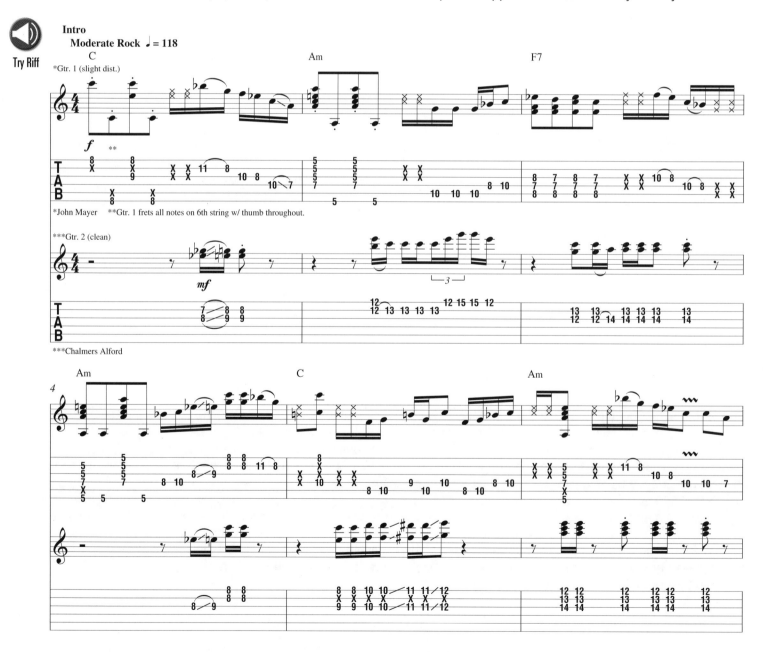

Who Did You Think I Was
From *Try!*, 2005

Where "Try" is primarily an improvised riff, "Who Did You Think I Was" is an excellent study in riff construction. The harmonic, rhythmic, and repetitive elements of the bluesy intro come together to form a definitive statement.

The intro is centered on a looping A7 vamp, once again mixing major and minor pentatonic sounds. The riff starts off with a root to a half-step tritone slide from the fifth-position A7 chord. The tritone, shown as white circles in the following chord grid, consists of a ♭7th/3rd interval (i.e., G/C♯ of the A7) and has the coolest, yet most callused, sound of the blues. As you slide the tritone shape, try to keep your thumb planted on the E string while pivoting from your wrist. This should take some slow practice as you keep the E string ringing through this next exercise. (If you experience pain—stop; you don't want to risk tendonitis!)

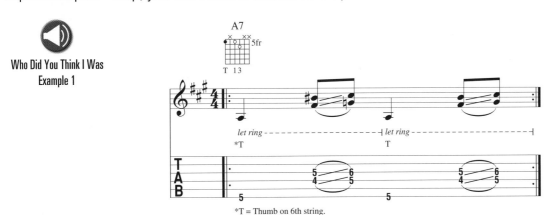

Beats 1 and 2 of each measure stay the same with a tritone slide and minor pentatonic single notes, but the tail end varies in unique ways to create a two-measure loop. In measure 1, he plays a C–G–C line after a couple of muted strums. Use a down–down–up picking pattern for the eighth–fifth–eighth fret on the E and D strings while you apply careful fret-hand muting. Using your pinky and index fingers for those frets, your hand will naturally fall in position for the minor pentatonic scale. Measure 2 streamlines the tail end by gradually bending the eighth fret and vibratoing the D note of the fifth fret of the A string. After the riff is played three times, the intro ends with what is essentially measure 1, except he articulates the A and G notes on beat 3 in lieu of muted strums.

The muting pretext is necessary for how aggressive his right hand is, as the constant strumming necessitates accuracy with fret-hand muting and alternate picking for the 16th notes. Check out the Integral Techniques chapter for more on controlling your aggressive picking with careful muting (page 108).

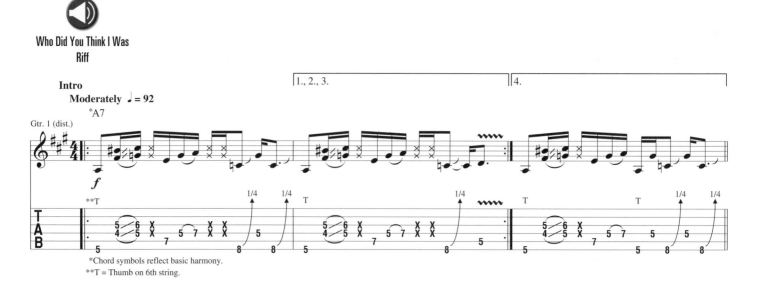

Who Did You Think I Was
Riff

*Chord symbols reflect basic harmony.
**T = Thumb on 6th string.

Waiting on the World to Change
From *Continuum*, 2006

A rationalization for nonintervention in an established order, the melancholy message of "Waiting on the World to Change" is bolstered by its bright, four-measure chord progression of D–Bm, G–D, A–Bm, G–D. The uplifting feel of this I–vi, IV–I, V–vi, IV–I sequence has been the cornerstone of feel-good pop since the '60s, and the brightness of the keyboard intro helps to embody that sentiment.

How John negotiates the rhythm and fills amidst the second-verse lyrics for added power is a great study in musical placement. Throughout, Gtr. 1 sparsely comps the changes with sixth-string-root chords, save for the D^V chord every other measure, which is most likely used for the economical fingering after the third-position G chord.

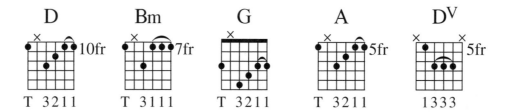

The rhythm he finds fits the pocket so well that he retains the rhythmic essence of the pattern throughout.

This framework lends itself to place the fills around the vocals on beats 3 and 4. Because each opportunity occurs over a Bm or D chord, he draws exclusively from the seventh-position B minor/D major pentatonic and remains sparse in note choice. But in measure 6, his subtlety is abandoned for a 16th-note triplet, legato line to catch your attention for the lyrics, "'cause when they own the information, oh, they can bend it all they want." Being placed when the central idea of the song is revealed, this aggressive lick serves as an excellent example of how less is more and that placement is more important than constant flash.

Waiting on the World to Change
Riff

Words and Music by John Mayer
Copyright © 2006 Specific Harm Music
All Rights Administered by Goodium Music, Inc., c/o Cal Financial Group, 700 Harris Street, Suite 201, Charlottesville, VA 22903
International Copyright Secured   All Rights Reserved

The Heart of Life
From *Continuum*, 2006

Centered on an optimistic view of humanity, "The Heart of Life" is a consolation for the downtrodden in times of hardship. The uplifting message is perfectly supported with effortless folk strumming and melodic fingerpicking. Finding a comfortable singing key, John tunes his guitar down a half step. If the riffs for "Neon" and "Something's Missing" haven't been motivation enough to buy an electronic tuner, follow the tuning tips from "Bold as Love" (page 36).

The main accompaniment pattern is a Paul McCartney-style, Travis picking riff with simple sixth-string-root chords. While the shapes are simple major and minor chords, the 6th, 7th, and sus4 suffixes help follow the melody by adding the pinky and index fingers. Before you tackle the rhythm, practice making the position shifts smooth.

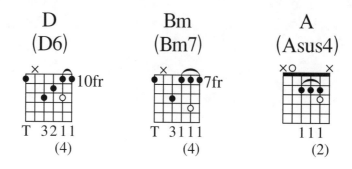

With the chords and shifts smoothly happening, let's get into the right hand's role of folk strumming. With this technique, you flick the dyad with your index finger as you slap your thumb down in between the plucking. The Integral Techniques chapter delves deeper into proper hand placement, plucking, etc., but give this next example a try.

**Heart of Life
Example 1**

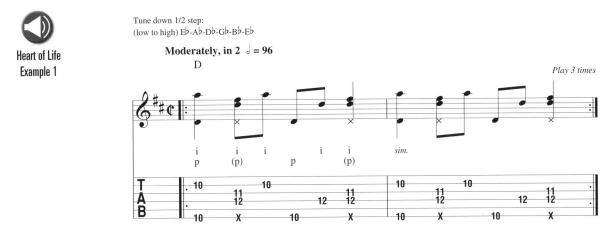

If you follow the plucking closely, you'll notice that beat 3 has consecutive *i* (index finger) notation. This can be tricky because you pluck the G string then flick the G string *again* with the index finger. The plucking motion actually sets you up for the flicking motion, so this is an elegant solution for smooth execution.

**Heart of Life
Riff**

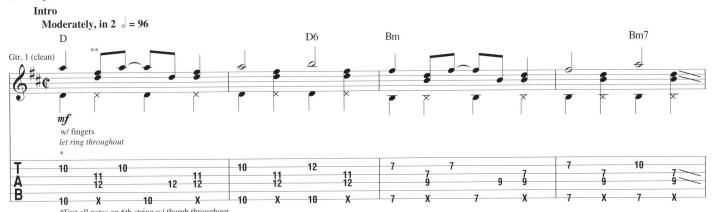

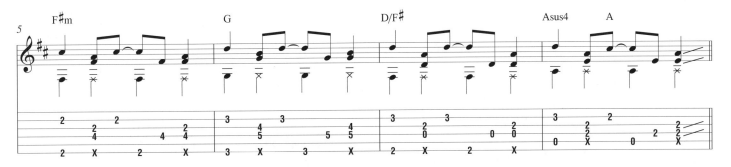

INTEGRAL TECHNIQUES

Ever the evolving artist, the scope of John's techniques has been far-reaching. From folk to blues, rhythm to lead, and acoustic to electric, he's incorporated the best of all worlds into his music—not only for their flash, but for their ability to heighten his expression on the instrument. His use of thumb fretting and fret-hand muting allows him to control string noise despite hard-hitting strums, his accompaniment techniques add dimension to his acoustic playing, and his lead style is an extension of his vocal delivery. Throughout this book, we've only hinted at how to perform these techniques, but this section will dig deeper into the specifics and shed a brighter light on how you can apply them with as much passion as Mayer.

Thumb Fretting

This technique, frowned on by classical players as unorthodox, is a mainstay in the styles of Jimi Hendrix, SRV, Eric Johnson, and of course, John Mayer. Classical players use all of their fingers for plucking the gut-strings of their guitars. Because they pluck the notes they want to play at moderate volumes, their need to compensate for controlling distortion is unnecessary. Blues and rock players, however, are tasked with controlling their loud distortion and hard-hitting strumming by any means necessary, so thumb fretting was naturally utilized.

The multiple reasons for the popularity are due to its use by the formidable innovators of 20th century popular music. Jimi Hendrix's over-the-top technique, absurdly loud amplifiers, and power trio ensemble were all controlled by his extremely large hands. His fingers had to be everywhere at once, as he was responsible for both harmony and solos, so the thumb was a logical addition to his style.

Another innovator whose thumb became an essential element to his artistry was Chet Atkins. Not only was his right-hand thumb crucial to his Travis picking, his constant basslines and simultaneous melodies benefitted from the added mobility that thumb fretting provides.

As evidence throughout this book, John Mayer used both of these reasons to his advantage. His Hendrix-sized hands and harmonic awareness on par with Chet Atkins serve his songs well. The wide stretches for the C#m11 and F#7b5 chords heard in "No Such Thing" and the moving basslines coupled with common tones in the main riff of "My Stupid Mouth" all owe their harmonic character to thumb fretting.

Now that we've fully explored the reasons to incorporate this under-used digit into your bag of tricks, let's outline the physical techniques needed to use it smoothly and—most important—safely.

To start out, let's examine how we fret the full-barre F chord. The index finger needs to press down across the entire first fret, even though strings 6, 2, and 1 only benefit from the pressure. This means there's wasted effort in barring strings 5–3. But if you use your thumb for the low E, you only need to worry about barring the top two strings. While this is simpler for your index finger, you need to curve your palm towards the guitar so your thumb can curl over the back of the neck.

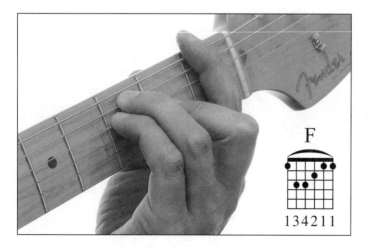

F

134211

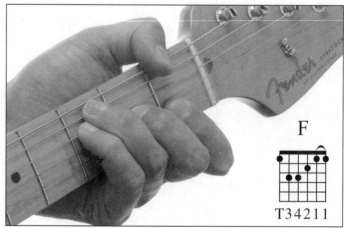

F

T34211

Similar to finding the sweet spot for your fingers' optimal tone and comfort, experiment with the following three options for where your thumb frets the string: on the joint, in between the joint and the tip, or on the tip itself. Give it a try with the following chords.

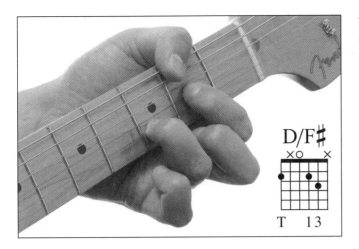

The D/F♯ chord begins to use the thumb on the same fret as your lowest finger, which allows fretting on the joint.

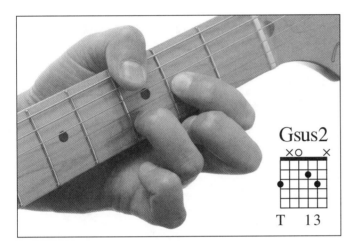

While the Gsus2 chord has the same fingering as the D/F♯ chord, where the index and ring fingers stay in place, the root is now on the third fret—the same fret as the ring finger. Here, the length between your thumb and ring finger begins to shorten, so you may have to choke up a little more.

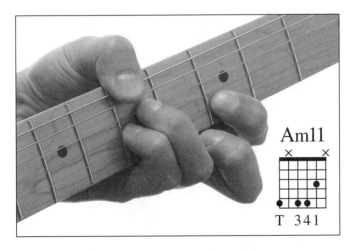

Am11 is the most challenging chord we've encountered when it comes to thumb fretting. The pinky is involved, so curling the palm towards the floor is needed, but the thumb compensates for it by fretting with the tip.

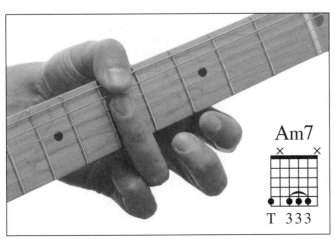

In comparison to the Am11 chord, let's see how this Am7 fingering makes things easier. Fret with the thumb and barre with the ring. It's interesting how we're only changing one note, but we're avoiding so much pain.

The thumb is not only a liberating chord-grabber, but it's also advantageous for wide-interval jumps in your lead lines. With your thumb over the back of the neck, the octave jumps in this self-contained riff maintain the implied E minor harmony as you make your way through the 12th-position pentatonic box.

Techniques
Example 1

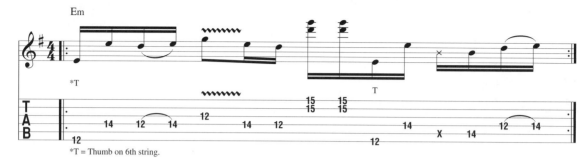

*T = Thumb on 6th string.

Fret-Hand Muting

An underlying texture of his style, Mayer's sense of rhythm is an undeniable constant of his artistry. His relentless right-hand motion results in a solid rhythmic feel. Because the right hand is constantly moving, where does the articulation come from? Well, it comes from *fret-hand muting*.

The interpretation of when to play aggressively is often missing from tabs, as most only show the dominant notes. Example A below demonstrates how a fret-hand muting example might be notated. But what is really heard is that C note with deadened notes surrounding it (Example B). The "Xs" are typically omitted for readability, but the underlying feel of this is the difference between '80s blues and '40s jazz.

Techniques
Example 2

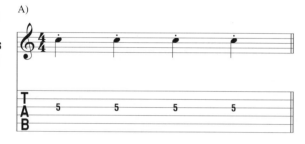
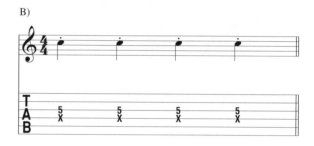

Fret-hand muting is a delicate balance between what is heard and where you pick. Back with that C note example, your pick ends at the target note. To get the percussive effect of fret-hand muting, you have to graze the string in front of it (i.e., mute the D string). But how do you mute the D string? Well, there are two strategies: you can mute with the tip of the finger that's holding the note…

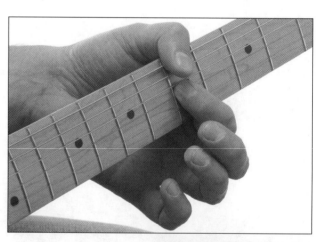

…or you can use another finger, like the index or ring, depending on the passage.

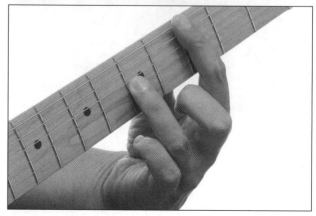

Before you start playing the licks in this book with that aggression, practice playing chromatically up one string while focusing on the sound, strumming accuracy, and fretting. Note that the open-E string is a unique case, because you're muting the surrounding strings only.

While the numbers below the tab suggest a one-finger-per-fret scheme that shifts up every fourth note, you should also practice using a single finger up the length of the string.

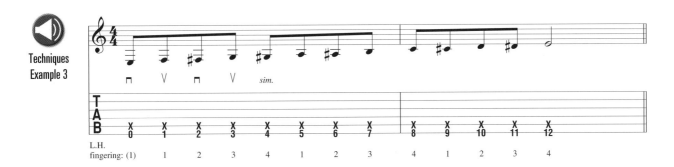

Techniques
Example 3

This next example skips a fret and then moves back one as you ascend the string. As you play, isolate which fingers allow ringing notes. From experience, the index and ring fingers are usually solid, but the under-used middle and pinky fingers often require more drilling repetitions.

Techniques
Example 4

While fret-hand muting on a single string is a great way to match the feel with the sound, let's use the fifth-position A minor pentatonic scale to get used to crossing strings. This drill moves up and down from the root to 5th (A to E) on the E and A strings, played in 16th notes. This is effective because the pinky gets high-intensity muting practice. With strict alternate picking, the upstrokes are also susceptible to error, so if you hear the open-G string, your strumming arch is too wide.

Techniques
Example 5

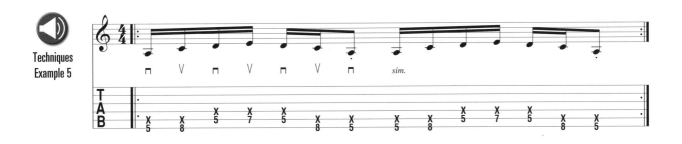

Expounding on the previous example, this two-beat riff moves up to the G string and back. Crossing strings is the trickiest part of the technique, so aim your pickstrokes to only sound the target fret and the muted string behind it.

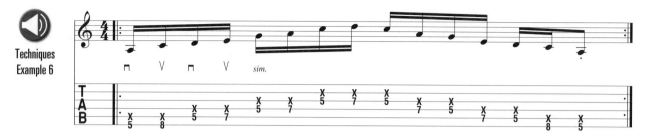

Techniques
Example 6

Remember, your left and right hand work in concert to balance the clear notes with muted noise, so use both finger angling and picking accuracy to help you achieve the muted sound that gives your lines the added power.

Accompaniment Techniques

Be it Travis picking with folk strumming, fingerpicking punctuated with acoustic planting, or thumb slapping as a rhythmic undercurrent of "Neon's" funky riff, John's wowed his listeners, both private and live, with only his voice and guitar in musically fulfilling ways through his various accompaniment techniques.

Because of his love for playing acoustic, he enhances his rhythms by simulating a backing band. While fingerpicking and/or strumming are both useful accompaniment styles, they don't have that percussive "oomph." So in order to create a driving groove in a solo setting, we'll add dead notes to beats 2 and 4 of each measure. Why? We're emulating a snare drum backbeat, and this important piece of the drum kit defines the groove.

There are three ways guitarists perform this simulation, and Mayer typically uses thumb slapping and folk strumming. Before we get into those, let's examine the simplest—acoustic planting.

Let's start with a basic fingerpicking progression. We'll use the following example as a basis for introducing our percussive techniques. This simple G–Am7, G/B–C progression anticipates each chord change but keeps the feeling of the pulse alive with root notes on the beat.

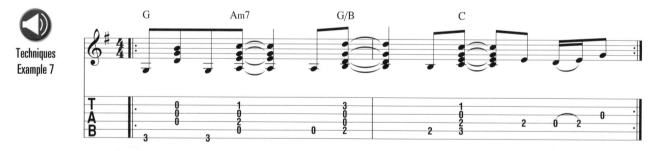

Techniques
Example 7

To liven up the groove, we add *acoustic planting* to beats 2 and 4. This involves moving our hand into position for the next chord with a little more force than normal. For this example, after you pluck the G chord on beat 1, bring your plucking fingers down on the strings (in preparation for the following Am7 chord) forcefully so you hear the strings slap against the frets.

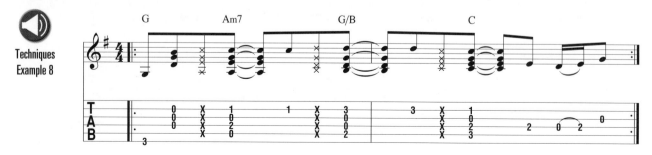

Techniques
Example 8

Thumb slapping involves hitting the string with the side of the thumb with an exaggerated wrist motion. The position of your right hand is important for the attack, so check out the photos below. As you can see in photo #1, the underside of your thumb creates a 45° angle with the tip that is resting on the string. With a little wrist action, the preparation of the attack moves your thumb several inches above the strings (photo #2). For the attack, bring your thumb back down to the E string. Once it makes contact, continue the motion through the string so it comes to rest on the one below it (photo #3).

Photo #1   *Photo #2*   *Photo #3*

Let's start by alternating the chords with slapping to get our hand in the groove. Try out the technique with this simple exercise, arpeggiating a G barre chord by exclusively alternating between a thumb slap and the index finger. Targeting the G string with your thumb requires demanding accuracy, so take this one slowly and focus on consistent execution.

Techniques
Example 9

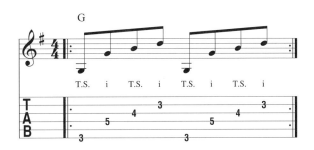

Now that the motion is under your hands, let's add some fingerpicking ideas. Inspired by the swung-16th groove of "Neon," this next riff kicks the tempo up, adds more chords, and keeps the alternation going where the thumb plays muted notes as the arpeggio heads down the strings.

Techniques
Example 10

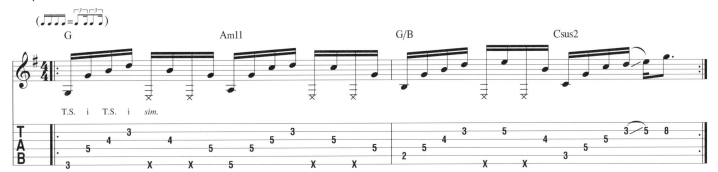

You may notice that some patterns are trickier to play with a consistent percussion sound. To remedy this, try moving your hand closer to the neck of the guitar. This gives you more leverage on the E string, allowing it to slap against the frets.

The final option for solo guitar percussion is *folk strumming*. Here, we simply strum the strings with the index finger—using a downward flicking motion toward the floor and/or upward strums—between plucked notes. The contrast between the strummed and plucked articulations creates the natural accents.

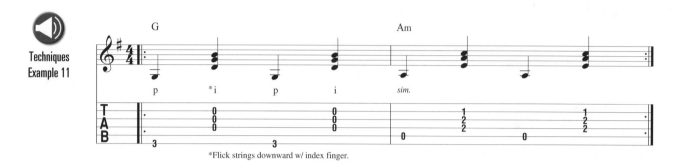

Adding single-note plucking creates the need for scripting out which finger does what. While the middle and ring fingers take care of the top three strings, the index finger sometimes pulls double-duty. So in this next example, check out measure 4, beat 3, in which you pluck and then strum with your index finger. This works well because the plucking motion primes the index finger into position for the strum.

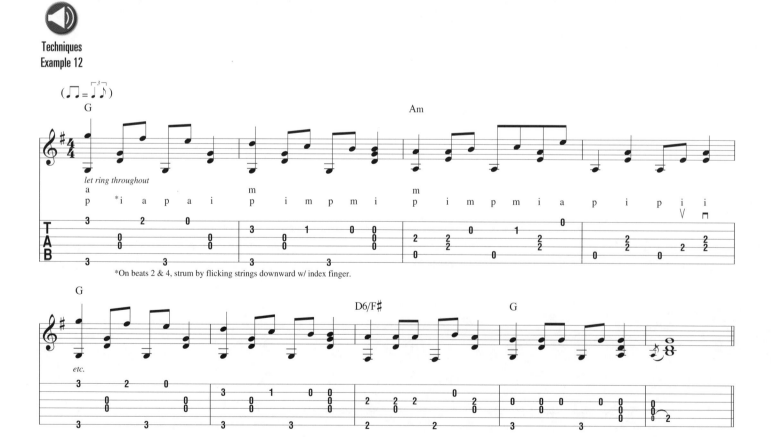

Pentatonic Articulations

Pentatonics are prime fodder for Mayer's improvisations in the blues and pop genres for which he writes. But, the nature of the shape creates unavoidable clichés when it's played in the standard box form. Here, we'll explore his methods for taking those five notes beyond convention into the realm of melodic soloing.

To make the sounds of those five notes all his own, John often eschews the very source of the clichés itself: the in-position box shape. Inherent to its form and how it's learned, the box shape instinctively triggers the blues-rock muscle memory of bending licks we've all heard before. How John completely avoids them is by playing the scale on only one string. This vertical versus horizontal method of playing the scale forces him to limit his ideas to sequential legato and lyrical bends. The solos from his studio recordings of "Gravity" and "Waiting on the World to Change" are perfect examples of these concepts at work.

The mapping of the neck is a requisite for developing melodies, so let's get used to playing scales on the B string. For the C major scale of this next example, take note that there are at most two frets (i.e., a *whole step*) between each note.

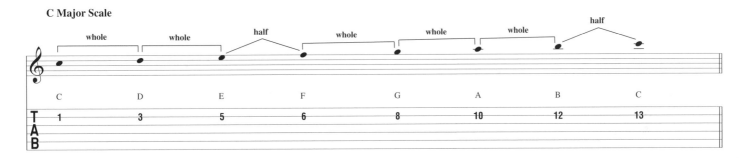

C Major Scale

Now, since the pentatonic scale has only five notes—as opposed to the major scale's seven—there are wider jumps from one note to the next (i.e., a minor 3rd). Playing the C major pentatonic scale on the B string makes this difference of intervals all the more obvious.

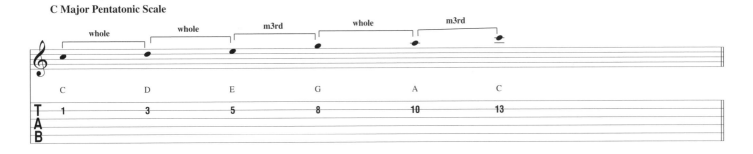

C Major Pentatonic Scale

Practice these on all strings by finding the root, keeping them within the first 12 frets. Because the C major and A minor pentatonics share the same notes, we're essentially playing the same scale at different starting points.

Techniques
Example 13

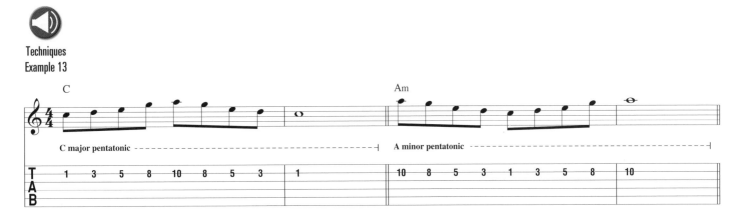

To firmly ingrain the scale intervals into your fingers, here's an example of playing parallel pentatonics on the same string. The structure of the major and minor pentatonics is different enough that the sounds rely on slightly altered intervallic formulas. D major pentatonic is a root–2nd–3rd–5th–6th pattern (D–E–F#–A–B), while D minor pentatonic is made of a Dm7 arpeggio with an added 4th (root–♭3rd–4th–5th–♭7th: D–F–G–A–C). Playing them back to back should build a stronger connection to the notes and their intervals.

Techniques
Example 14

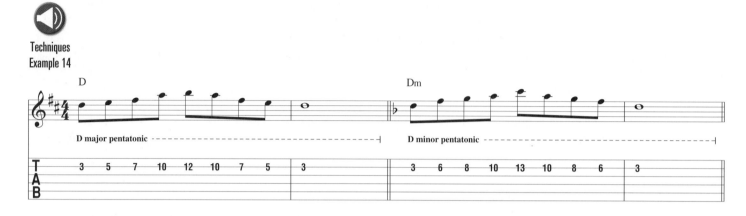

Now that you're used to moving up and down the string, let's practice them by adding bends to the C# minor pentatonic scale. Here is a sequential descent through the scale on the B string where a sliding and bending pattern articulate the same notes. The slides are first in order to get the sound in your ears for the bends. This aural preparation will particularly come in handy for the 1-1/2-step bend in measure 2.

Techniques
Example 15

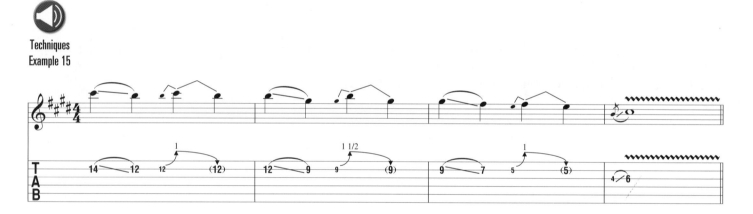

This next example complicates things by adding sliding legato to the bending maneuvers. After the bending descent, this lick caps with a pull-off/sliding ascent to the 12th position. All the slides are performed with the ring finger, but make sure that the 14–17 slide on beat 2, measure 3 stays in rhythm.

Techniques
Example 16

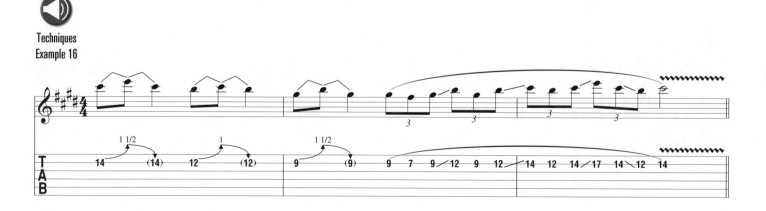

Fingerpicking Lead Lines

As a contrast to his aggressive rhythmic approach to soloing, John often uses his fingers, in lieu of the pick, to enhance the more intimate moments of his live performances. Not only do the fingers help avoid the potential technical pitfalls to which alternate picking is prone, they can help control the tone of your lines by varying how hard you pluck the strings.

To suit his live playing needs and at a moment's notice, he magically rolls the pick between the knuckles of his index and middle fingers.

Because of this placement, the plucking motion used with the index finger must come from the joint or from the wrist, as you pull away from the guitar. Experiment with the following licks, taking special consideration for the double stops.

Technical

For single-note lines, he alternates his thumb and other fingers, typically the middle and ring. Play through the sliding C/E arpeggio that opens the lick with a sweeping motion of your thumb for the D and G strings, following it up with the middle and ring. The next three-note pattern is the main reason using the fingers works great: you can use a repeating p–m–a fingering, but if you picked it, the down and upstrokes would flip-flop every beat, causing weird string crossings as a result.

Techniques
Example 17

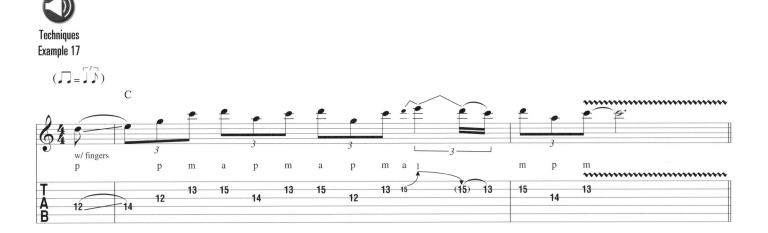

Double stops are also a great showcase for fingerpicking. Similar to the string crossing that it helps avoid, you can easily play two notes at the same time with the middle and ring fingers.

The following major pentatonic lick uses hammered double stops followed by a lower string as it descends through various inversions of a G chord. The shift from the 14th to 12th position requires nimble work from your fretting hand, so use your index/middle for the 14th/15th-fret double stop, then after your pinky addresses the 17th fret, D string for the final time, quickly shift back to the 12th fret, barring with your index.

Techniques
Example 18

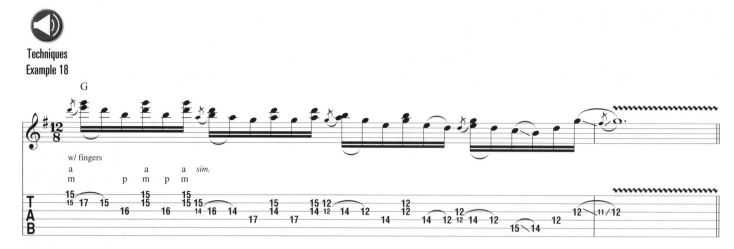

Try both of the previous licks with alternate picking to hear and feel the simplicity that using your fingers affords.

Subtlety

Not only are most technical problems avoided, the fingers' direct contact with the strings allows for a wider palette of expression—namely *dynamics.*

Let's use a derivative of the previous double-stop lick to explore this concept. Dynamics refers to how loud or soft a note is played, and John uses this quality of music to a passionately expressive end. The next example repeats the same six-note pattern while gradually decreasing in volume. To do this, simply pluck the strings lighter and lighter for each repetition. You'll notice the difference in tone and feel.

Techniques
Example 19

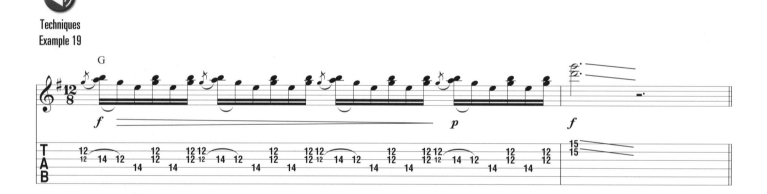

Speaking of changes in tone, another possibility is the contrast between picking and plucking the same note. In measure 2 of this Albert King-inspired lick, play the first whole-step bend with your pick; then play that same note with your middle finger by popping it. The drastic, piercing sound of the popped note is significant in conjuring the pain of the blues. Finish the bending series with your middle finger as it sets you up to downpick the B string.

Techniques
Example 20

STYLISTIC DNA

While Mayer's impressive array of technical inclusions are bombastic displays that draw you in, his reasons for using them are often overlooked because of their deliberate and effective application. Here, we'll dissect the "why and when" of where he places his techniques.

Chord Extensions

Chord extensions add harmonic richness to your rhythm playing, and John uses them for multiple effects. In songs like "No Such Thing," "My Stupid Mouth," "Daughters," "83," etc., he uses them for enhancing a static harmony, melodic voice leading, and consistent common tones over supposedly non-related chords. A grounding in music theory would heighten all aspects of your musicianship, but there are ways to get these sounds without an expensive college degree.

The easiest way is to incorporate open strings into your chords. Taking a generally simple harmony (like power chords) and adding open strings to them will magically transform their sonic quality, especially on acoustic. The following chords are based on the fifth-string power chord shape with ringing open strings on top. Strum through them as you move up the neck to see if any spark a new song idea.

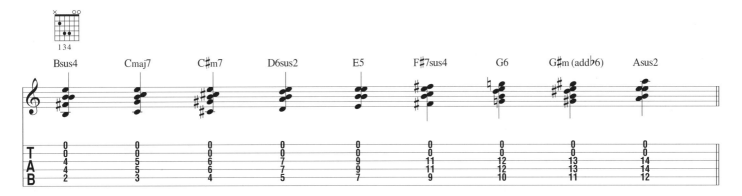

While the chords in the above example have a pleasing side to their sound, the next example has three chords that are a little harder to stomach—the reason being that there are half steps between more than one of the notes of the chord, while the previous eight have whole steps or scale tones that fit their harmony. Even the chord names themselves sound complicated. When you strum through them, the half steps that are so close to the roots of the chord are responsible for the clashes.

These chords are built from B♭5, D♯5, and F5 (shown in parentheses), and each one of the roots are a half step away from the open B and E strings. You would've been able to tell that these chords sound rough if you cycled the chord shape up the neck fret by fret.

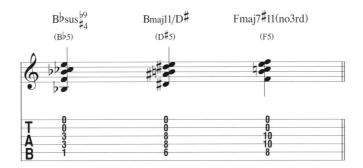

Another possibility is fourth-string roots. The pre-chorus from "No Such Thing" uses this to great effect with power chords. The same rules concerning half steps apply, so experiment accordingly.

A little bit more restrictive of a rule are diatonic 3rd shapes from the E and B scales (both major and minor). Here are the 3rd shapes from the E major scale on the D and G strings.

The following example strums and arpeggiates through the 3rd shapes, creating harp-like sustain via the open and fretted strings.

DNA
Example 1

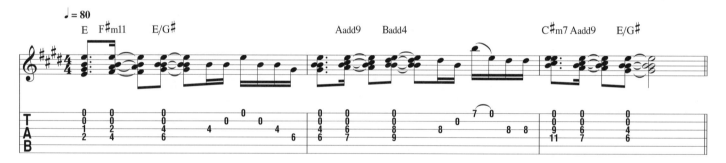

Pretty much any scale that has the same letter as the open string you use fits. Say you want to explore the open A string; experiment with chords and riffs from the A major or minor scales, keeping the open string as a drone.

There are other options for experimentation. Let your ears be your guide as you experiment.

Move suspended and open-string chords up the neck and maintain the root notes as you move the shapes. Csus2 and Gadd9 are unique in that the open strings are on the inside of the fretted notes.

Change one note from a barre chord (up/down a fret, substitute with an open string, etc.).

The rest is up to you...

Starting Phrases on Offbeats

Taken from his jazz influence, John often uses hammer-ons and slides to address chord changes from a whole or half step below. Where the majority of players start their phrases on beat 1, starting phrases on the offbeats also breaks up the predictability of your solos. In order for the chord tones to land on the beat, he starts his lines just before the downbeat of the measure and then slurs into the chord for a harmonically strong phrase.

To do this, he outlines the arpeggio he's on by approaching it via scale tones from the song's key center. If we're in the key of G, for example, playing over a C chord, he might use these respective scale and arpeggio shapes to construct an ascending line.

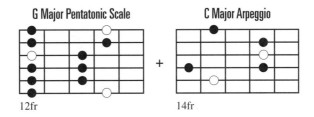

Inspired by his live solos, this C arpeggio line hammers and slides its way from 12th to 15th position through G major scale approach tones. The slides make easy work of the position shifts, but use your index and ring fingers for the slides at the 11th and 16th frets, respectively. The lick then climaxes at the 20th fret, E string with a bend/release move back to the 15th fret (G), followed by a walkup to the anticipated 19th fret (B: 3rd of G). The ring-finger bend-to-index-finger pull-off in measure 2 is quite a stretch, so move your hand down the neck for the pull-off to smoothly access the 15th fret.

DNA
Example 2

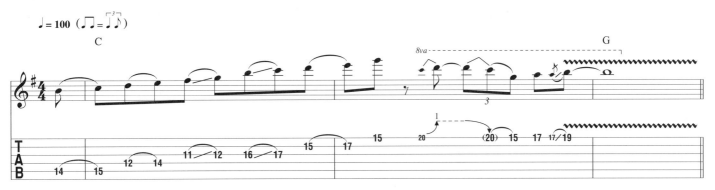

Thematic Repetition

Thematic repetition is a common device John uses to build the melodic sections of his solos. One of the advantages of repetition is that you can get a lot of mileage out of a simple idea. The following is a C major pentatonic lick that features a gradually ascending series of bends amidst an A–C–D walkup. The walkup grounds the extremities of the eventual overbends and creates wider intervallic jumps from the D, as a result. Use your ring finger with ample support for the bends and be prepared to smoothly make the shift from the 15th fret to the bending fret on the B string, as it changes each time.

DNA
Example 3

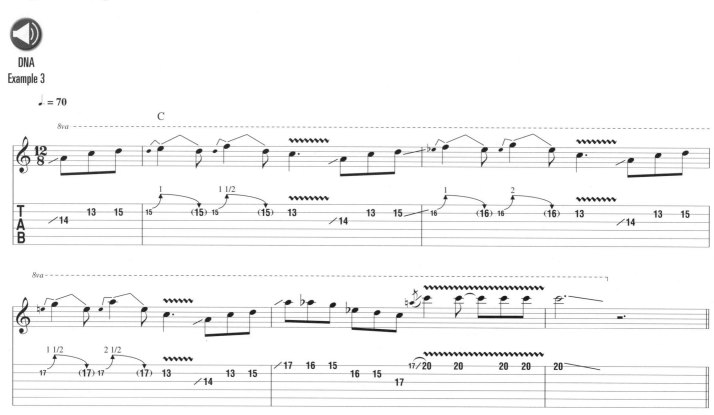

Compacting the idea of repetition into a smaller fragment, this lick relies on rhythmic variations for its intrigue. Here we have a three-note pattern in C minor pentatonic played in an even 16th-note rhythm, which creates unexpected accents across the measure. While the top note of the separately picked unison bend (G) alternates from the ♭7th to the root (B♭ to C), the accented bends create the variable forward motion, because of the juxtaposition of odd patterns and even rhythms.

DNA
Example 4

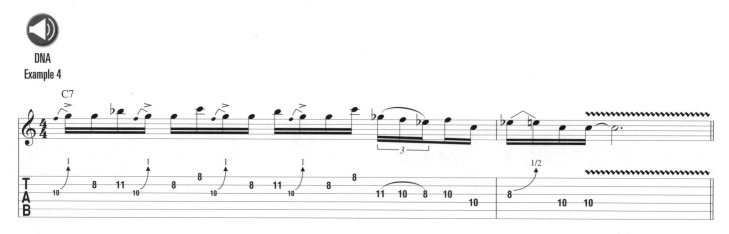

Stating a lick and then developing it into a larger idea can serve as the motivic glue that holds a solo together. It also gives the listener something to hold on to, lulling them into the mindset that they can predict the direction your solo will take. But when you add a technical or rhythmic surprise at the right moment, their ears will perk up, bewildered by the contrast of the simple and technical. The management and manipulation of your listener's expectations is the de facto role of the soloist, and thematic repetition is a sure-fire way to keep them guessing.

Vocal-Like Devices

The highest achievement for any guitar player is to have a sound so recognizable that it can be associated with them within one or two notes: B.B.'s "hummingbird" vibrato, Albert King's litany of bends, Clapton's "woman tone," etc., are all signals that a truly great bluesman has his hands on the instrument. Notice that these are all subtle things, unique to each one of them but pleasing to all. Your sensitivity to things like vibrato, phrasing, sustain, staccato, etc., can be elements that make up your style. Mayer, being an expressively soulful singer, relies on the vocal quality of bends and slides in unexpected places to enhance his melodic statements.

He uses back-to-back bends in his bluesy phrasing, possibly as an homage to T-Bone Walker. This next lick features whole-step bends from both the ring and index fingers, creating a lyrical E–D–C descending line on the G string. Perform the ring-finger bend at the seventh fret as normal, pushing up with support from the middle and index fingers. Since the index-finger bend at the fifth fret doesn't have bending support, pull the string *down* towards the floor, using your forearm muscle for the action (with a little help from "gravity" as well). Also, be sure to slowly release each bend in rhythm, as that retains the vocal-like sound of the technique.

DNA
Example 5

While the bends are a physically demanding example of smooth changes in pitch, applying slides and vibrato to would-be held notes is a subtler device towards the allusion of anatomical note production.

Here's a run-of-the-mill lick that the average pentatonic soloist would struggle through with gobs of distortion. While it sounds OK, it certainly lacks personality because the bends and vibrato are in the places you'd normally expect from the pentatonic box.

DNA
Example 6

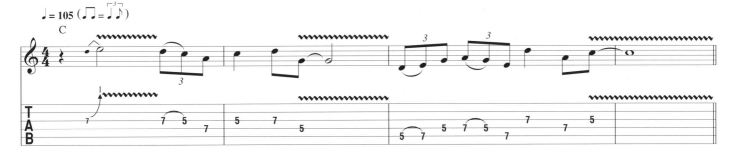

Here's an expansion of that idea, dressed up with a variety of slides. Measures 1 and 2 are the most obvious of departures, where the pick attacks are cut in half and almost every note is approached via a whole-step slide. The variety of articulations adds a subtle quirkiness to a line that would otherwise sound boorishly uninspired.

DNA
Example 7

Beat 4, measure 3 of the previous example touched on the idea of sliding to the same repeated note. Exploiting the same sustain quality of the bend-slide maneuver we learned in the Essential Licks chapter, it can't be understated how the slide technique adds unconventional character. This lick uses it as more of a position shift, making ready for the hammer-on to a whole-step bend. Once you slide through the C/E arpeggio, play the 10th fret, B string with your ring finger; then, instantly slide up to it from the eighth fret with your index finger. Keep the sustain going with a little vibrato and then hammer on to the 15th fret, bending it the whole step, all in one fluidly legato motion. The final hammer-on is a bit of stretch if you keep your index finger planted, so let the 10th fret go as you reach for the whole-step bend.

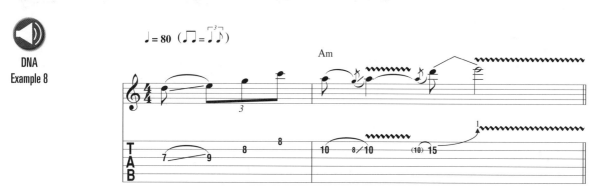

DNA
Example 8

Solo Construction

Now it's time to put all the ideas together. Over a minor-style blues in D, we'll construct a dynamic solo on top of a Hendrix-style rhythm part. The solo is a repeated, four-measure progression of Dm–C, B♭–A, Dm–C, B♭–C–Dm, so the D blues scale (minor pentatonic with ♭5th) works perfectly. The pacing and flow of the solo is what we'll focus on, as John Mayer's melodic/technical approach to shaping his ideas is distinctive. The concepts explored in this section are particularly inspired by his solo in "Slow Dancing in a Burning Room," so playing these solos back to back can be a study in applying those ideas to your own improvisations.

The first four measures of this solo are restricted to primarily a melodic descent on the B string with bends and grace-note slides. Use your ring finger for each bend, except for the 11th fret in measure 3. The similar rhythmic phrasing of measures 1–2 and 3–4 is a great device for thematic repetition and pacing for a solo's ebb and flow. Notice how the accents differ; the first measure accents the downbeats, and the second measure accents the chord change.

Measures 5–8 bring in the technical influences and blues vocabulary but still retain a melodic slant. The tart bend to the C note, serving as the ♭7th of Dm and the root of C, is syncopated with delayed attacks and shaken violently through measure 5. The gradual release is then followed by a chromatic descent, approaching the A note from above and below with half-step slides and bends. Use your ring finger for all the activity in measures 5–6, save for the 13th-fret pull-off.

The position-blurring legato of measure 7 adds technical interest with split-second rakes that address various inversions of a Dm7 chord. Get the feel for the lick by omitting the rakes and focusing on smooth position shifting, adding them back in as icing on the cake. Once you're ready for the rakes, practice fretting the chords, as bracketed in the notation, and then loop the rake and legato moves that follow.

The solo closes with an in-position, double-stop climb towards a bending barrage of the 5th and ending with the root. To smoothly play the pair of notes at the 12th fret, use your middle finger for the D string and then switch to your ring for the G-string bend. The pull-off to the 10th fret then frees your ring finger to grab the bend at fret 13, capping the solo with sustained vibrato.

As you can see and hear, repetition with similar material are prime ingredients for a melodic opening statement, and technical ideas featuring unique rhythmic phrasing all add up to a satisfying musical outing. Learn these concepts well, and you'll be on your way to soloing John Mayer-style.

DNA
Example 9

MUST HEAR

All the examples in this book are inspired by his inaugural *Room for Squares* through to his confident *Battle Studies*, so particular footnotes will be paid to recommendations from his later efforts.

Room for Squares, 2001
Essential Tracks

No Such Thing
Why Georgia
My Stupid Mouth
Your Body Is a Wonderland

Heavier Things, 2003
Essential Tracks

Bigger Than My Body
Come Back to Bed
Something's Missing
Daughters

As/Is, 2004
Essential Tracks

Covered in Rain

Try!, 2005
Essential Tracks

Try!
Who Did You Think I Was

Continuum, 2006
Essential Tracks

Waiting on the World to Change
Gravity
Slow Dancing in a Burning Room
Bold as Love

Battle Studies, 2009

Essential Tracks

Who Says
Perfectly Lonely
Assassin
Crossroads
Friends, Lovers or Nothing

Born and Raised, 2012

During his three-year dry spell of musical output since *Battle Studies*, John's troubled public life and vocal surgery found him recovering and finding solace in the heart of Montana. Where *Continuum* is a result of Mayer's refreshed batteries for the popular song structure after his blues-trio album *Try!*, *Born and Raised* is a rootsy re-immersion into his passion for Americana, where he takes advantage of simpler arrangements and country-style instruments for a more song-oriented approach in the vein of Neil Young, Bob Dylan, and Crosby, Stills & Nash.

Essential Tracks

Queen of California
Shadow Days
Face to Call Home

Paradise Valley, 2013

Essential Tracks

Wildfire
Paper Doll